Look at That Bird!

Look at That Bird!

A Young Naturalist's Guide to Pacific Northwest Birding

Karen DeWitz

little bigfoot
an imprint of sasquatch books
seattle, wa

I dedicate this book to my patient and supportive family, and to the next generation of Northwest birders. Get out there, and enjoy our region's amazing wildlife!

Printed Manufactured in China by C&C Offset Printing Co. Ltd.
Shenzhen, Guangdong Province, in December 2020

LITTLE BIGFOOT with colophon is a registered trademark of Penguin Random House LLC

25 24 23 22 21   9 8 7 6 5 4 3 2 1

Editors: Christy Cox, Michelle McCann
Production editor: Rachelle Longé McGhee
Designer: Tony Ong
Interior illustrations and photographs:
    Musical birdsong notation (pages 28–29): Delaney Pearson
    European robin photograph (page 49): Maddy Reid
    Illustrated crow and raven tails (page 89) and bone identification chart (page 159):
        Cary Porter (http://coreshadow.blogspot.com)

Library of Congress Cataloging-in-Publication Data
Names: DeWitz, Karen, author.
Title: Look at that bird! : a young naturalist's guide to Pacific northwest
    birding / Karen DeWitz.
Description: Seattle : Sasquatch Books, [2021] | Includes index. |
    Audience: Ages 8–12 | Audience: Grades 4–6
Identifiers: LCCN 2020027397 | ISBN 9781632173171 (paperback)
Subjects: LCSH: Bird watching–Northwest, Pacific–Juvenile literature. |
    Bird watchers–Northwest, Pacific–Guidebooks–Juvenile literature.
Classification: LCC QL683.N75 D49 2021 | DDC 598.072/34795–dc23
LC record available at https://lccn.loc.gov/2020027397

ISBN: 978-1-63217-317-1

Sasquatch Books
1904 Third Avenue, Suite 710
Seattle, WA 98101

SasquatchBooks.com

Contents

Red-breasted sapsucker

Welcome to the World of Birding!

What is the fastest animal on Earth? What can swallow its dinner whole and then spit out the bones? What animals do scientists say are the closest modern relatives of extinct dinosaurs? One class of animals is the answer to all those questions and more. They're all birds! Who knew? Read about each of these birds later in this book to answer all of the above questions and more.

From upper left: juvenile barred owl, pileated woodpecker, peregrine falcon

How to Use This Book

This guide is written specially for beginning birders in the Pacific Northwest. Every bird included is one you might see in your own yard or during your adventures in nearby natural areas (or even cities in some cases).

Northern flicker

The book is divided into two parts. The first section tells you about birds in general and shows you things you can look for to help find and identify different species. Read it to learn about the cool features that make birds different from every other animal.

The second section is a field guide to many of the common birds living in the Pacific Northwest. A field guide is a type of book you can take with you to identify plants, animals, and natural features out in the field—in nature.

Birdwatchers (birders) are called ornithologists when they're studying birds for science. Both hobby birders and ornithologists often keep lists of all the different birds they've spotted in their lifetime. These lists are known as life lists (or lifer lists).

As you look through the birds in this book, think about starting your own life list. How many of these birds have you already seen? Think of the birds here as your starter set. Adding more is part of the fun!

American crow

As you learn to tell bird species apart, keep an eye out for a few individuals that come back to visit you over a summer or even over several seasons. There are crows, for example, who come back to visit their favorite people year after year. Some even bring gifts to their human friends—everything from cones to pebbles to sparkly trash they find in their daily wandering.

This little downy woodpecker has an adorable field mark that makes him easy to recognize: the red patch on the back of his head looks like a heart!

How to Be a Birder

Identifying Birds

To be a birder, you'll want to learn to identify the birds you see. Start by noticing basic features like a bird's general size and color. Then you're probably going to need to check out a few more details to make an identification. Those details are called field marks. They are the little physical features—marks, patterns, and accent colors—that help identify a particular type of bird. As you look at the birds in the field guide section of this book,

Look for individuals in your usual birding spots. This little female Anna's hummingbird arrived at the feeder with a broken bill. For many species this could spell catastrophe, but this little gal was a fighter. Literally. She defended "her" feeder from all other hummingbirds and successfully raised a family that year. Her broken beak didn't hold her back at all!

you will read about different field marks to look for in addition to details about where you might find the bird and how it might sound.

Using Bird Blinds

One way some birders catch sight of shy birds in the wild is to use a hiding place called a bird blind. It can be as simple as a bunch of branches placed to conceal you, or as complex as an actual building covered with grasses or other natural materials. You can sometimes find permanent bird blinds in wildlife refuges where people go to birdwatch.

Bird blind

Whether or not you have a bird blind, you should consider wearing clothing that will help you blend in with your surroundings so birds are less likely to see you. This is called camouflage. Wear muted natural colors that help you blend into the area where you'll be. If you wear your hot-pink hoodie to the forest, you can be sure the birds will see *you*, but odds are you won't see *them*. Take a lesson from birds. Not only do they often have coloring that camouflages their bodies, but they also construct their nests with materials that blend in with the surroundings so predators won't see them.

Brown creeper

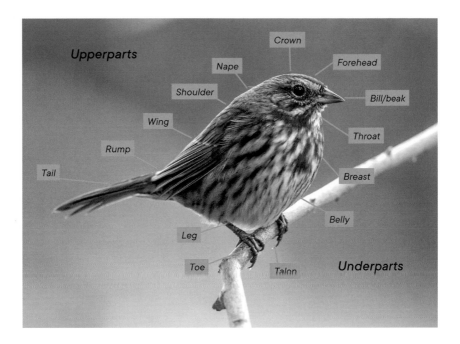

Upperparts

Crown

Nape

Forehead

Shoulder

Bill/beak

Wing

Throat

Rump

Tail

Breast

Belly

Leg

Toe

Talon

Underparts

What Makes a Bird a Bird?

Birds have parts we don't have (like wings), and they are missing some that we do (like teeth). Here's a quick look at bird body parts.

Parts of a Bird

This photo shows some of the most common body parts birders notice when they're looking for field marks on a bird. If you know what each part is called, it makes it easier to explain to other birders what you saw.

Bones

You can't actually see the bones, but they're a big part of what makes birds able to do what they do. Birds are vertebrates, which means they have a backbone and skeleton like people do. But unlike people, birds have bones that are thin and mostly hollow. This helps make them light so they can fly. Putting feathers on a bird-sized human wouldn't be enough to turn a person into a flier. (People have tried, though!)

Who knew? It looks like birds' knees bend backward, but that part isn't actually their knee. It's their ankle! Birds' knees are usually hidden by feathers up near their body. That long bone that comes down forward from the backward-bent part is actually what would be a foot bone on a human.

The knee is hidden up under the robin's wing.

This is actually more like an ankle than a knee.

Crops and Gizzards

This Steller's jay's full crop shows how much food it's saving for later.

Other internal parts that allow birds to do what they do are the crop and the gizzard. Not all birds have a crop, but it can be a big help to those that do. The crop is a pouch in the throat where a bird can temporarily store extra food.

This lets birds gather more food at one time than they can eat. Bird parents can also store food in their crop, then regurgitate it later for their babies to eat.

Instead of having teeth like humans and other animals, birds have an extra part to their stomach that helps them grind up the big pieces of food (or even whole animals) that they swallow. That second stomach is called the gizzard.

When a bird swallows food, it goes down the esophagus to the first part of the stomach (a lot like a human stomach), where stomach juices start the process of digestion. Then the food enters the second side of the stomach: the gizzard. The gizzard squeezes and churns the food that's been eaten, rubbing it against tiny rocks and other grit the bird has swallowed. (Yes, birds swallow little rocks and grit on purpose!) This breaks down the food even more so it's ready for the intestines. Imagine how fast you could eat if your stomach chewed your food for you!

Juvenile Canada geese (goslings)

Who knew? Pigeons and doves can do something extra-special with their crop. They produce a substance called crop milk that they can feed to their babies. It's not actually milk like you may be imagining—only mammals can make that. But crop milk is pretty amazing. It's full of important fats and proteins. Scientists have learned that it is extremely nutritious and helps baby birds grow quickly, even if it's fed to baby birds who aren't pigeons or doves.

Poop

All animals poop, but have you ever wondered why bird poop looks so much different from the poop of other animals? Believe it or not, that white stuff helps birds to be lighter, just like their hollow bones. Unlike humans, birds don't have a bladder to hold urine (pee). All that liquid would just be too heavy when they're flying. Instead, birds produce that same waste as a white paste that goes out with their poop. That's why bird poop has both brown and white parts to it. It's also why

Anna's hummingbird

bird poop is so hard to wash off. That white stuff is made up of something called uric acid, which doesn't dissolve in water very well.

Who knew? In places where a lot of seabirds gather, their poop can build up into thick layers, like around these Brandt's cormorants nesting in cliffs along the Oregon coast. Long ago, humans discovered they could use that built-up white stuff, called guano, as a natural fertilizer for their crops and gardens. Guano is an important resource that many countries around the world trade like other crops.

Feathers

Feathers are the first thing most people notice about birds, and that makes them a great place to start when you're trying to make an identification.

FEATHER COLOR AND PATTERN: What color are the bird's feathers? Are there any markings on them? Is there a pattern or design? Are there spots or streaks? Thinking about these questions can help you figure out what kind of bird you're seeing.

Who knew? Blue bird feathers don't actually have any blue pigment in them at all. *Then what makes them look blue?* The color blue in feathers is a lot like the blue of the sky or the ocean. Water isn't actually blue. It's clear, but it looks blue sometimes. The blue color is produced by the way light hits the feathers themselves. Those feathers are structured in a way that makes blue light reflect

back while the other colors cancel each other out. What does that mean? Don't try to make blue ink by grinding up blue feathers. If you break down the structure of the feather, the blue goes away.

FEATHER TEXTURE: If a bird's outer feathers are all fluffy and stick out funny, you can make a good guess that it's a juvenile (not yet a mature adult). Bird feathers usually get sleeker and flatter as they get older. All birds have fluffy feathers underneath, though. That's called down, and it's what keeps them warm in the winter.

Baby birds grow through a few different phases, and their feathers usually look different at every phase. That can sometimes make them tricky to identify. Keep an eye out for parents nearby to help you learn which baby goes with which species.

Look at the feathers on these two great horned owls. The bird on the left is an adult. Even though it's pretty fluffy (it was cold that day), it has sleek flight feathers and shows the typical brown-and-white pattern of that species. The bird on the right looks like a giant fluff ball. That's a baby owl, also called an owlet. It hasn't grown its flight feathers yet, but it has lots of down to keep it warm while its mom and dad hunt to keep it fed.

Here are some examples of how baby birds may look in three different phases of development—hatchling, nestling, and fledgling—and what feathers might look like during these phases.

HATCHLING: A hatchling is a newly hatched baby bird. Some hatchlings come out of their eggs almost naked except for a few pin feathers along their spine. Pin feathers are feathers that aren't yet developed. You can mostly just see the shaft (the center "trunk" of the feather), so each one looks like a straight pin. Babies hatched like this are totally helpless and depend on their parents to keep them warm and fed. Other babies, such as chickens and ducks, come out covered in soft, fluffy down. Species that hatch covered in downy feathers are often ready to wander around with their parents right away. They learn how to find their own food much sooner than birds who hatch naked.

Hummingbird hatchlings

NESTLING: A nestling is a slightly older baby bird who is still too young to leave the nest. Nestlings don't have their flight feathers yet and are often patchy and downy as different types of feathers start growing in. If you ever find a nestling or hatchling lying on the ground (they can't fly and will look pretty helpless), ask an adult to look for a nest nearby and put the baby back. Ignore popular myths that say the mama bird will ignore

American robin nestlings

the baby if she smells your scent on it. Birds want their babies to survive and will welcome a fallen nestling back into the nest.

Barn swallow fledgling

FLEDGLING: A fledgling is a young bird who has left the nest but may not yet know how to fly. They will often look a lot like their parents—complete with at least partially grown tail and wing feathers—but are quite a bit fluffier. This is the kind of baby bird you are most likely to see in the wild. These are also the baby birds many people think they're rescuing by taking them in when they find them on the ground. The "rescuers" mean well, but don't do that! If a bird looks old enough that it might be learning to fly (even if it can't fly yet), leave it alone and check to see if there's a parent nearby. Fledglings spend a lot of time flapping around on the ground learning how to be birds. Let them do that without any help from people.

Look for these fluffy young birds in the spring and summer, when most birds lay their eggs and raise their broods (families). If you're lucky, you might see an adult bird feed a fledgling. Sometimes that fledgling has a body that's already about as big as its parent! Some fledglings can be even a bit *heavier* than their parents after being fattened up, giving them the best possible chance after they leave the nest.

Fledglings of many species will fluff themselves up with their mouths wide open and shake their wings to get their mom's or dad's attention. Bird parents can't pass up a wide-open mouth. Some have even been known to feed babies who aren't their own!

Red-breasted nuthatch adult (right) and fledglings (left and center)

Look at how close in size these two birds are. You'd never guess one was a baby unless you saw it begging to be fed. In some species, baby birds hardly look like their parents at all. They can be different colors, different sizes, and even have different-colored eyes. Eventually—sometimes years later—the juveniles start to look more like adults. Patterns, feather color, and even eye color can change as a juvenile bird grows into an adult.

Starling fledgling (left) and adult (right)

If you find a feather on the ground, look at it carefully. What part of the bird do you think it came from? Scientists have a lot of different names for the specific types of feathers on a bird, but it's good to just notice broader categories when you're first really looking at feathers.

Long, sleek wing feathers look very different from fluffy down. Tail feathers look different from the feathers on the sides of the body. Even tail and wing feathers look different if you look closely. A tail feather has a shaft that goes right down the middle, dividing it in two. A wing feather has the shaft over to one side, so the two halves aren't the same size. The United States Fish and Wildlife Service has a great website where you can identify feathers. Go to www.fws.gov/lab/featheratlas to learn more.

Body feather

Down

Tail feather

Wing feather

After you've looked at a feather, place it back on the ground where you found it. Go ahead and take a picture first if you want to keep a collection or do more research at home, but you should leave the feather behind. Believe it or not, it's actually illegal to collect most feathers from wild birds. The law helps protect birds from people who might want to hunt them for their feathers. It's simpler to make a law against owning or keeping the feathers at all than to figure out who found theirs lying on the ground and who took theirs directly from the birds. Basically, you can only collect feathers from birds you can legally hunt.

Who knew? Birds are the only living animals on Earth that have feathers. But scientists now believe that many dinosaurs were also feathered. Look at a great blue heron or pileated woodpecker and squint your eyes. Can you picture their dinosaur ancestors? Yup, birds and dinosaurs are related!

Great blue heron

Sometimes animals—including birds—don't come out looking exactly how we expect them to. In some cases, it's like some of their feathers forgot to turn on the color switch. Animals that have patches (or whole bodies) of white where they should have color are described as being leucistic (pronounced "loo-sis-tick").

This white bird is actually a leucistic American robin. Identifying a bird like this is like recognizing an animal in a coloring book. The outlines are familiar, so you can figure it out from there without all the usual color and pattern clues. Unusual versions of common birds are great finds for a birder.

MOLTING: When a bird loses its old, worn-out feathers and grows new ones, it's called molting. It's a little like when your dog or cat sheds its old fur. Most birds molt yearly. Some birds also do a partial molt just for breeding season. These birds have a muted look part of the year but put on bright, flashy colors when it's time to attract a mate.

American crow

They go back to a less colorful appearance once they have babies to raise (and keep hidden).

These molting differences can make some birds challenging to identify—especially when they are in the process of switching out their feathers—but that can be part of the fun of birding. Every bird sighting is a new puzzle to figure out.

PREENING: In addition to helping most birds fly, feathers also keep them warm and dry. Feathers are an important adaptation (a physical feature or a behavior that helps an animal survive in the wild), so birds have to take good care of them. They do this with a combination of oils (for waterproofing) and regular cleaning and combing—all using just their beaks and their feet. Many birds produce oil in a gland near their tail that they spread with their beaks to waterproof their feathers. Birds also use their beaks to pick mites and dirt from their feathers, keeping them clean, healthy, and strong. They flatten out or move feathers that have gotten ruffled out of place—like when you comb or brush

Anna's hummingbird

your hair—using both their beaks and their feet. All of this feather care is called preening, and it's one of the bird behaviors you're likely to see in the wild.

Who knew? Some birds—such as jays and crows—do something odd as part of their feather care that ornithologists call anting. They either sit on an ant hill and let the insects crawl all over their feathers, or they actually grab ants with their bills and rub them on their bodies. One theory is that the acid in ants (called formic acid) helps the birds get rid of mites and lice.

WINTER FLUFFINESS: When the weather turns chilly, birds puff up their feathers to trap pockets of air inside. It's the same reason you may wear a puffy coat in the wintertime. That trapped air is warmed by the bird's body heat and helps to protect it against the cold. Birds will often tuck one foot up inside the feathers to get it warm too. Then when the other leg gets cold, they'll switch feet. Another adaptation birds have to keep their feet warm is that the vessel that brings warm blood from the heart is right next to the one that brings cold blood back into the body. So the blood from the feet gets warmed up before it reaches the rest of the bird.

Chickadee

Check out this little dark-eyed junco. Can you spot its right leg? If you look closely, you can just see a few toes peeking out from its belly feathers.

Birds keep their feathers in shape the same way you take care of your hair: by taking a bath. This can be a fun bird activity to observe at local ponds and lakes, or even in a backyard birdbath. You may be concerned if you see a bird flopping around in the dirt. But don't worry! Many birds, including the sparrow (top right), like to take dust baths. The dust helps soak up oil in the bird's feathers to keep them in top condition.

Look closely at a feather. Each feather has a center shaft like the trunk of a tree. There are branches coming out from the central shaft that are hooked together with tiny barbs, like a zipper. Sometimes the little barbs come unhooked, so the "branches" get unzipped. Rezipping those closed is one of the bird's jobs when it's preening.

Feet

Bird feet can tell you a lot about how a bird spends its time. Watch to see if the feet are made for perching, climbing, hunting, or swimming.

PERCHING: Long, sharp toes that grab a branch or twig, like these crow's feet, are for perching. Most songbirds—from the tiniest bushtit up to the loudest crow or raven—have perching feet. They're made to grip branches and twigs while the birds sing, watch for threats, or hunt for food.

Perching feet (American crow)

CLIMBING: The sharp claws on a woodpecker help it hold on to the side of a tree. A woodpecker will often swoop down onto a tree trunk and then hop up or down its side with both feet. Imagine if you had to hop two-footed up the side of a tree using only your toenails to hold on! Many perching birds also use their sharp claws and long toes for climbing.

Climbing feet (hairy woodpecker)

HUNTING: Big, strong talons are made for grabbing prey (animals hunted and eaten by other animals). Talons are sharp, hooked claws at the end of a bird's toes. Check out the talons on this immature bald eagle! It's not even fully grown yet, and those sharp claws are already lethal weapons. They're not only extremely sharp,

Hunting feet (juvenile bald eagle)

but they are also amazingly strong. Birds of prey use their powerful talons to pierce into their prey and carry it to their young or even just to a better eating spot.

SWIMMING: Webbed feet are made for swimming. They push against the water to help birds move easily across and through it. Geese, ducks, and gulls have webbed feet to help them swim on the ponds, lakes, rivers, and oceans where they make their homes. If you see a new bird you don't recognize and notice it has

Swimming feet (gull)

webbed feet, you can be sure that it's some kind of waterbird.

Beaks

Beaks (also known as bills) are made of a combination of bone and keratin. Keratin is the same stuff that makes up human hair, fingernails, and toenails, as well as birds' feathers. The shape of a bird's beak can tell you a lot about what it eats. There are many different types of beaks, and learning a few of the most common in the Pacific Northwest will help you to get started recognizing the birds you see here.

NECTAR-EATING: These are long, thin beaks that let a bird drink nectar (natural sugar water) from deep inside a flower or feeder. Nectar-eating beaks, like the Anna's hummingbird's pictured here, may look like straws, but birds don't actually suck up liquid like we do. Check out the hum-

Nectar-eating (Anna's hummingbird)

mingbirds on page 132 to find out more about how these amazing birds use their bills to get food.

INSECT-EATING: There are many different types of beaks that belong to insect eaters, and all of them have special qualities that help birds catch their tiny prey.

Birds that catch flying insects out of the air have mouths that open wide like a net. This northern rough-winged swallow caught a

Insect-eating (northern rough-winged swallow)

whole mouthful of goodies for its babies by flying low over the surface of a slow-moving river. Its beak is extra wide just for that purpose.

Probably the best-known insect eater of all—the woodpecker—has a long, sharp beak that not only grabs bugs to eat but also works like a chisel to dig holes in wood to find the hidden treats inside.

Insect-eating (hairy woodpecker)

MEAT-EATING: Birds of prey (the meat eaters) have strong, hooked beaks with sharp edges. They use their beaks to tear chunks of meat from their prey.

Check out the powerful beak on this bald eagle! That turned down hook at the end is a classic meat eater's bill shape.

Meat-eating (bald eagle)

SEED-EATING: Seed-eating beaks are thick and strong to crack through tough seeds and nuts. The size of its beak tells you the size of the food a bird usually eats. If you see a bird with a great big strong beak, you'd better believe it's hoping for the biggest, crunch-iest birdseed you can provide.

This female black-headed grosbeak's triangle-shaped beak is perfect for cracking open seeds and nuts.

Seed-eating (black-headed grosbeak)

WATER-FEEDING: Birds that find their food in or near water often have beaks either for hunting or for straining water as they consume small plants and animals.

Some water-feeding beaks help the bird catch and eat fish. These beaks are like spears—long and pointy. This great blue heron uses its long, sharp bill to grab or even stab fish and other small animals (such as crayfish and frogs) from wetlands. After it catches a fish, a heron will flip it up in the air until it's positioned right so the bird can gulp it down whole.

Other water-feeding birds, like this mallard duck, have flat beaks that are perfect for straining small edible goodies out of a pond. Even baby ducks use their bills to strain plants, insects, worms, and other food from pond water. Unlike some birds who are fed by their parents for several weeks, baby ducks are ready to start using their bills to grab food from the pond right from the start.

Water-feeding (great blue heron)

Water-feeding (mallard duckling)

Don't let those duck bills fool you though. Many ducks do their fair share of hunting too. Hooded mergansers enjoy lamprey, crawdads, and other small water-dwelling critters. (Learn more about mergansers on page 95.)

One of the brightest parts of a baby bird is often its gape. This is the term ornithologists use to describe the wide-open, brightly colored mouth of a baby bird. At the base of the beak, you can see folds of soft tissue that look a bit like human lips. That's called the gape flange, and it lets babies open up really wide for feedings—all the better to attract a parent's attention! As a bird gets older, its gape usually gets less colorful and the gape flange loses its flexibility.

Bird Talk

Sometimes the best way to discover birds in your area is to simply be quiet and *listen*. Some birds sing songs, often to mark their territory or attract a mate. In addition to songs, which are usually (but not always) longer and more complicated than their other sounds, birds also have a variety of calls that they use to communicate. They can make an amazing array of shorter chirps, whistles, coos, hoots, and trills to quickly send warnings and other information to each other.

If a bird is looking for a mate, there's a call for that. If a bird wants to warn its friends that a threat is nearby, there's a call for that too. When you hear the same sounds over and over, you can begin to notice which birds are nearby when the sounds are made. This is how you can start to pair different

birds with their sounds. It's great to try this near your home or in a park you go to often since you're likely to see and hear the same birds over time.

There are a number of online sources that you can use to identify a bird's call. The Cornell Lab of Ornithology's All About Birds website and the National Audubon Society's website are good places to start.

You may not be able to read music, but on the next two pages, look at the way the notes of each bird's song go up and down. That shows you that the tone of the song goes up and down. In other types of bird songs, the notes are clustered really close together all in a row. That represents a trill—a type of song where the bird's voice flicks back and forth between one or two high notes so quickly that it makes one long, connected sound. Think of how a coach's silver whistle sounds when it's blown kind of softly so it rattles.

Black-capped Chickadee

Do you hear a bird with a call that sounds a little like "chick-a-dee-dee-dee"? Look closely for a tiny gray, tan, and black bird with a short, thin beak. It's called a black-capped chickadee. You might even see its brown-vested cousin, the chestnut-backed chickadee (see page 70). Just keep your ears open for them calling their name: "chick-a-dee-dee-dee"!

American Robin

Some people describe the robin's song as sounding like "cheerily, cheer up, cheer up, cheerily, cheer up." Their call is a sharper cheep-ing sound.

Dark-eyed Junco

A dark-eyed junco song is a trill (like a sports coach whistle), and it's loud enough that it can sometimes be heard up to 100 feet away. When they call to each other, juncos make a sort of short chipping sound, like "cht-cht-cht."

Who knew? In as many as four out of every ten songbird species, only the males actually sing. Some scientists believe not singing allows females to save their energy for laying eggs and nesting. *Why else might female birds not sing?*

Sandhill cranes

Alert! Alert! Alert! Did you know you can never scare off just *one* bird in a flock? When you scare a single bird, you scare them all. Birds alert to warn others of a threat nearby. Some of that warning is transmitted through a sound like a screech, click, chirp, or click. Some is transmitted by their body movements. Think of how you might react if you saw someone flinch near you. Would you look around to see the threat? Would you flinch too?

Some birds even have different calls for different types of threats. They can tell their flock if the threat comes from the land or the sky, for example. When a bird is startled, its panic spreads to nearby birds—even birds and animals of another species—like the ripples on a pond when you throw in a rock. When you walk out into nature, do you ever hear a sharp call or two and then . . . nothing? That's the birds alerting each other to *you.*

Where to Find Birds in Your Area

Birdwatching is a great hobby because you can find birds just about everywhere. Even the most crowded cities have feathered residents— pigeons, crows, sparrows, and even falcons. If you want to see a wide variety of birds in one place, try visiting a natural area containing wetlands. You can even make a trip to one of the many national wildlife refuges scattered around the Pacific Northwest. These amazing places are filled with diverse wildlife and often have helpful staff to answer questions and point you toward interesting birding spots. Some of them even have binoculars and field guides you can check out for free while you visit!

How to Attract Birds to Your Yard

To bring birds to your own yard, you need to think about what all animals need to live: food, water, and shelter.

You can provide food through feeders as well as by planting native plants that birds like to eat. Research carefully before you plant anything new in your yard. Will it help or harm the birds? Some common decorative plants are actually toxic if

American goldfinch (left) and chestnut-backed chickadee (right)

they're eaten. Birds are usually smart enough to avoid them, but if other food is scarce, it could be a problem.

As for ways to provide food, there are many types of feeders out there, each suited to a different type of food for different types of birds. It's a good idea to have a variety of feeders in your yard. That way you can attract many different kinds of birds and let them separate out a little by size and type.

You can also provide water for birds to use for drinking and bathing by adding a fountain or a birdbath to your yard. Be sure that you keep the water clean so the birds stay healthy. Old, dirty water can be a breeding ground for mold, bacteria, and even mosquitoes. Sprinklers for your lawn can attract birds too, especially if the spray hits low-hanging plants and trees. If you look carefully, you may see little birds flapping around for a bath in the wet leaves.

Red-breasted nuthatch

This crow is using the birdbath to dunk and soften chunks of dry bread. It will eat some and take some back to its nest—a snack and a drink in one!

Shelter is another issue to consider when attracting birds to your yard. Many birds like the protection of bushes, brambles, and nearby trees. You can also add birdhouses and perches to give your feathered friends a reason to stay for a while after they've visited for a snack, a sip, and a bath.

Birds typically roost (settle in for the night to sleep) in trees or on rocks, or in other places where they feel safe. The word *roost* is also used to describe where a bird sleeps. Most birds only use birdhouses (nesting boxes) and nests while they are caring for eggs and babies. Make sure any nesting boxes you put out are clean and ready to go well before mating season. And make sure there are other safe places for birds to roost if you want to see them in your yard when that season (spring and early summer for most Pacific Northwest birds) has passed.

Who knew? Many birds have developed a remarkable adaptation for sleeping. They can sleep with one eye open and keep half of their brain awake! This lets them keep an eye out (literally) for predators while getting some rest. Birds can actually choose which side of the brain rests, or they can rest both sides if they're feeling especially safe.

You can help local nesting birds by loading a clean suet basket feeder, an extra kitchen whisk, or even an old hairbrush with clean straw, wool, animal fur, or natural unbleached cotton. Many bird species will come to the stash to find soft linings for their nests. Just make sure anything you put out is free of pesticides or anything else that could be toxic to birds. Also, don't put out long pieces of human hair, yarn, or other types of string that are hard to break. Birds can get tangled up in those, and many times they're made of materials that don't break down over time. It's better to let birds use grasses, thin twigs, and rootlets for the longer pieces of their nests.

Rufous hummingbird female

CATS: INSIDE IS BEST!

As you start to attract more birds to your yard, think about what you can do to help them visit safely. In some cases, that means thinking about how your pets (or wandering neighbor animals) may affect your new bird friends.

Cats, in particular, like to roam around their neighborhoods looking for critters to hunt and little trophies to bring back to their families. But all these roaming house cats are really bad for birds. Cats kill *billions* of birds in the United States every single year (even more than scientists thought just a few years ago). If you want to help the birds in your area, make sure you keep your kitty indoors or in a special "catio" (enclosed outdoor space). It's safer for the cat too!

You Can Do It: Suet!

Many woodpeckers love suet.

Suet is a great treat for birds (especially in the wintertime), and it's easy to make at home. When you make your own, you avoid all of the single-use plastic trays and packaging that usually come with store-bought suet. This recipe makes about five slabs of suet. Suet feeders look like little cages, and you can buy them at many grocery or general stores.

YOU'LL NEED:

5 empty and clean half-gallon milk cartons or other square molds (see Note)

2 cups squishy fat (shortening, lard, or rendered fat)

1 cup crunchy nut or seed butter (I use peanut butter)

3½ cups birdseed

1 cup uncooked quick oats

½ cup cracked corn (it's in the pet food section)

1 Cut the bottom inch or so off of each milk carton to make a shallow open box. Set these aside. You will use them as molds after you've mixed your suet. Recycle the scraps.

NOTE: You can also use plastic or silicone lunchbox sandwich containers, the empty trays from store-bought suet, small pans, or even old ice-cube trays as molds. You just want something you can freeze that will make a shape that fits into your suet feeder.

2 Put the fat and nut butter in a large glass mixing bowl. Microwave for 1 to 2 minutes so it melts a little and gets soft. It doesn't need to be totally liquid.

3 Mix in the remaining ingredients. Stir well so everything is coated in fat and nut butter.

4 Scoop the mixture into the milk carton molds. Smooth it down with the back of your spoon until the top of the suet is mostly flat.

5 Put the filled suet molds in the freezer for a couple of hours. You can even store them there if you don't want to put them all out in your yard at once. When you're ready to feed the birds, peel the suet out of the mold and place it in a suet feeder basket.

6 Wait and watch!

What kinds of birds visit your suet feeder? You can add them to your life list!

Canada geese

Migration

You've heard of birds flying south for the winter, right? That's one example of something called migration. While some birds stay in the Pacific Northwest all year long, others migrate or travel through on their way to other places. That means some of the birds profiled in this book will be around whenever you feel like looking. But others will fly away—sometimes thousands of miles away—for part of the year to feed or reproduce. You have to spot those birds while they're in town. The field guide part of this book will point out when you can see each bird profiled here. It's always a good idea to note what season you see any new bird. That will help you find an identification, and it will help you know when to look for it again.

Tree swallows are summer migrants to the Pacific Northwest.

Most of the migrating birds covered in this book go from north to south during the fall and winter. That means if you live farther south in the Pacific Northwest, you might still see some migrating birds that left the more northern areas weeks or even months before.

The good news is, since much of the Pacific Northwest has a mild climate, we have a lot of birds who stick around all year. A fantastic way to get a good look at

Steller's jay

local birds is to put out some feeders (especially suet) during the winter or early spring, and then make yourself a warm nest in a covered area nearby to watch. It may take a little while for the birds to realize you aren't a threat, but once they do, the time you spend sitting quietly will be well worth it.

When it's warmer outside, grab your binoculars and head to a nearby birding hot spot. You can find those places using resources such as eBird online.

eBird (ebird.org) is a giant, worldwide group science project for birders and scientists alike. It's an online collection of birders' observations while watching birds. Anyone—even you!—can report bird species to eBird. All of that data is then available for scientists and other birders, who can see when and where birds are spotted on eBird's maps. You can go online and look up a certain bird to see where it's been seen in your area. You can also look up a particular birding location to find a list of all the birds that have been spotted there.

Who knew? Many birds migrate at night. They fly overhead while the weather is cool and their regular predators are sleeping. Some of these giant flying crowds are even visible on weather radar. Humans can help keep these travelers safe by limiting the lights they shine at night, which can confuse the birds. We also need to make sure our glass surfaces are made bird-safe. (See more about preventing bird window strikes on page 204.)

Choosing and Using Binoculars for Birding

Binoculars are a tool that can help birders zoom in on the birds they spot to better identify a bird or see something special like a mother bird feeding her nestlings.

Choosing

There are many different types of binoculars. As far as what kind you choose, that all depends on you. If you're just starting out, inexpensive kids' binoculars will give you a taste of what binoculars can do for you as a birder. If you (or your parents) are willing to invest a little more, there are a lot of small binoculars made for adult birders that will work great for you in the field.

When you buy binoculars, you can choose both the magnification (how much bigger it makes things)—such as 8× or 10×—and the size of each lens, such as 32 mm or 42 mm. Kids usually do best with smaller lenses.

Using

Using binoculars seems like a no-brainer, right? You just put them up to your eyes and look. But it's important to take a few steps before you go out birding so you can actually see what you want to see through

them. Fiddling with your binoculars out in the woods is a great way to miss a cool bird that's been spotted nearby.

STEP 1: FIT THEM TO YOUR FACE. Look through your binoculars. Next, adjust the width of the eye holes to perfectly match the width of your eyes. If you do this right, you should see one big circle when you look through the binoculars instead of two overlapping circles.

STEP 2: FOCUS. Point the binoculars at something across your yard or street and turn the focus wheel between the two eye holes until

the object looks clear to you. Some binoculars will even have a fine-tuning adjuster for each eye. If you have this, close one eye at a time and fine-tune the focus for the open eye. When you open both eyes together, what you see through your binoculars should be crystal clear and pop out almost like a three-dimensional picture.

STEP 3: FIND SOMETHING COOL TO SPOT. If you walk around looking up at trees with your binoculars, you're likely to miss a lot of birds and maybe even trip and fall. Instead, learn to look for birds with your binoculars at your side or hanging from your neck by a strap. Then lift up the binoculars to look more closely at the birds you see as you walk around.

With your bare eyes, look for a bird or some other target you can use to practice spotting with your binoculars. Lock your eyes on that with your binoculars held away from your face. Then bring the binoculars up to your face without moving your head.

Did you easily spot your target? Practice until you can do the spotting quickly and easily.

Now you're ready to head out birding!

A Birder's Pledge

I promise to . . .

- Think about how my actions will affect the birds. Am I scaring them, leading predators to their nest, or driving parents from their chicks?

- Remember that every action I take in the wild is multiplied by the number of people who go there before and after me. It's not just me. It's millions of me.

- Let the birds decide how close to be. They can touch me, but I shouldn't try to touch or chase them. I will respect their space.

- Watch chicks from a distance. Often there is an adult bird nearby who is also watching and making sure the baby is okay. If I think a baby bird may be in trouble, I will find an adult who can contact a bird rescue organization.

- Respect private property and shared natural spaces. I will always ask for permission before tracking a bird onto somebody else's land. I will consider the people and wildlife around me while I enjoy natural parks and wild places.

Common Birds of the Pacific Northwest

In this field guide you'll find some of the most common birds from around the Pacific Northwest. It won't include every bird you might see, but you have a really good chance of seeing every bird in this book.

Each entry includes fun facts about the species and specific information to help you identify that bird.

SIZE: Size is one of the first things you'll notice about a bird that will help you identify a species, so this information is listed first in each entry.

COLOR & PATTERN: Color and pattern are the next most important things to look for to identify a bird. In some cases the color and/or pattern is different between the male and the female (sometimes *really* different). Each bird description will tell you when to look for something different between the male and the female. If a difference isn't noted and there's only one picture of a bird at the start of the section, then the male and female of the species look the same.

SOUND: You'll often hear many birds way before you spot them, and their sounds can help you locate them. Always keep your eyes *and* ears open when you're birding. You'll quickly learn a few common bird sounds and may be able to identify them without seeing them at all.

This book will give you a little bit of information about eggs and nests, but you should treat that part of birding with special care. It's not best for birds to have birders searching for their nests while they're in use. If you hunt for eggs and nests, you could scare off the bird parents or lead predators to the babies. The best time to look for nests is actually when they're not in use—in the winter after the leaves have fallen off the trees. You can often spot nests easily then (they won't be hidden in the leaves of trees and bushes), and you won't endanger the birds or their babies. Pictures of nests, eggs, or chicks included in this book were taken with great care by a professional using bird blinds and/or with hidden cameras or long lenses.

NEST & EGGS: This information covers the basic description of the nest and where it's built, as well as information about eggs, like the size of the clutch (a group of eggs produced by a bird at one time). Keep in mind that most birds only use their nests when they are laying eggs and raising young. The rest of the year, they just find somewhere comfy to roost.

FOOD: This entry tells you what each bird likes best to eat. This can help you find a type of bird or make an identification. For example, if you know a bird is a fish eater, you are more likely to find it if you visit a body of water. Or if you see a bird eating seeds, you can identify it more easily if you know which birds like to eat seeds, such as finches or sparrows.

REGION & HABITAT: All birds profiled in this book can be found in the Pacific Northwest, but they may also live in a wider region. This entry will include their full region. It will also help you identify a bird by its habitat, which is where you will most likely find a species of bird within a region. For example, some birds like forests. Others only live in deserts or wetlands. Some birds are more common along the coast, while others can be found inland.

SEASON: This information will help you know *when* you'll be most likely to spot a particular bird species. Some birds are migrators who are only here for the summer or winter. Others live here year-round.

Dark-eyed junco

American Robin

American robins are a common songbird that many people can recognize even if they're not birders. You can see robins in yards, parks, forests, and even cities. They often gather in big groups called flocks, especially in the winter.

Male

SIZE: American robins are a medium sized bird, between 8 and 11 inches long. They are so midsized and common, in fact, that they're often used as a comparison size by birders. When you see robins, pay special attention to their size, because it can help you categorize other birds. You can ask yourself, *Is this bird bigger or smaller than a robin?*

Female

COLOR & PATTERN: Adult American robins are grayish brown with orange underparts, and birds on the West Coast are lighter than birds on the East Coast. With robins, females can be lighter colored than males, but they aren't easy to tell apart unless there's a pair together that you can compare. Juveniles are often paler than the adults and have spotting on their back and chest.

SOUND: American robins are one of the most recognizable and common bird singers in the Pacific Northwest. They sing, call, and make other sounds that tell birders a robin is nearby. See more about robin sounds on page 28.

NEST & EGGS: Picture a bird's nest in your mind. Got it? You're probably picturing an American robin's nest. The female robin builds her cup-shaped nest out of dead grass, moss, mud, and twigs. The nest is usually hidden among the leaves in the lower branches of a tree, but some-times she'll make her nest on a  human structure, like the gutter of a house. Robins usually have three to five eggs per clutch, and they can have up to three clutches per year. Robin's eggs are well known for being a pretty sky-blue color, and you can sometimes find eggshells under the nest after the babies hatch.

FOOD: American robins eat insects, worms, and fruit. Interestingly, they're more likely to eat worms for break-fast and fruit for dinner. Maybe they heard the old saying, "The early bird gets the worm." When you see a robin searching for worms and grubs on the lawn, watch the way it moves: Hop, hop, hop, *freeze*. Hop, hop, hop, *freeze*. When it freezes, it will stare at the ground with its head cocked to one side as it looks for insect or worm movement. When it sees something, it'll peck its beak swiftly toward the ground to snag its prey.

REGION & HABITAT: American robins are found pretty much everywhere in North America. They love open grasslands (fields, yards, etc.), but they can also be found in the forest.

SEASON: Many people think of American robins as the first sign of spring, but they actually live here in the Pacific Northwest all year long. In fact, sometimes they're easier to spot in the winter because there are no leaves to hide them on the trees where they perch. Also, that's when you're most likely to see them in large flocks. If you live up in Alaska or northern Canada away from the coast, you'll want to look for robins in the summertime.

When settlers first came to the New World from England, they looked at a bird hopping around on the ground looking for worms and said, "Hey! That looks a lot like the little robin we have back home! We should call it a robin." It turns out, though, European robins and American robins aren't even close to the same kind of bird. What differences can you spot between this little guy and the American robin above?

European robin

Bald Eagle

Bald eagles are raptors, which is another name for a bird of prey. They are called birds of prey because they feast on small animals (their *prey*). All raptors have large, sharp talons on their feet and hooked beaks that they use to grab and tear their food. The talons and beaks on eagles are some of the sharpest and most powerful in the animal kingdom.

Raptors—especially eagles—are also known for their amazing eyesight. Eagle vision is four to five times sharper than average human eyes. Not only can they see farther, but their color vision is better than that of humans. Eagles and other raptors can see colors outside the spectrum (like the rainbow) seen by humans.

SIZE: Bald eagles are one of the largest birds in North America. They range from 28 to 39 inches long, and their wingspan can reach over 6½ feet. In birds of prey, the female is usually bigger than the male.

COLOR & PATTERN: First of all, bald eagles aren't really bald. (If you want to see a truly bald bird, check out the turkey vulture on page 187.) Instead, adult bald eagles—male and female—have white heads and tails that gleam brightly in the sunlight. The "bald" part of their name comes from the word *piebald*, which means "black and white." The rest of their body feathers are dark brown, and their beaks and legs are bright yellow. Juvenile bald eagles don't look like their parents until they're about four or five years old. Instead, they are almost completely dark brown with flecks of white throughout. That can make the identification kind of tricky for a birder.

SOUND: Surprisingly, bald eagles have kind of squeaky and unimpressive cries, especially when you consider how big they are. Bald eagle calls are high-pitched and whistling. The call sounds a little like "ki-ki-ki-ki-ki-ki-ker."

NEST & EGGS: Bald eagles build what may be the largest nests in the world. Made mostly of sticks, these giant homes are placed way up high in the tallest evergreen trees. They can be 2 to 4 feet deep and 4 to 6 feet wide on average. Eagles often return to the same nest year after year, and they often add on to the nest when they come back.

Researchers have found nests as big as 9 feet across! Bald eagles lay one to three eggs per clutch, once a year. The babies—called eaglets—hatch out covered in gray fuzzy down.

FOOD: Bald eagles are birds of prey. They really like fish, but they'll hunt and eat whatever's available. They are what scientists call opportunistic eaters, which means they'll take whatever they can with the least amount of effort. For example, they'll often steal other animals' prey or eat the flesh from dead animals (carrion) they find lying on the ground.

REGION & HABITAT: Bald eagles are found all over the United States and Canada. They like big, tall evergreen trees near bodies of water. Dinner and a view!

SEASON: In some parts of the United States and Canada, bald eagles migrate south or west during the colder months. Here in the Pacific Northwest, though, we can see bald eagles year-round. In the winter, bald eagles gather together in large groups to feed and roost. In the summer, you're much more likely to see them solo or in pairs.

The bald eagle may be best known for being the national bird of the United States, but did you know that we once came close to killing them off here? Shooting, habitat destruction, and pesticide poisoning all made it hard for these impressive raptors to thrive. In the 1960s, there were fewer than 500 nesting pairs of bald eagles left in the lower forty-eight states (not counting Alaska and Hawaii). Fortunately, we changed our behavior and our laws to save them before it was too late. They were listed as endangered for decades. That means they were close to going extinct in the wild. Now they are one of America's greatest animal comeback stories. They are doing so well that they have been taken off of the official endangered species list.

All parts of the bald eagle are still protected by federal law in the United States. You can't even legally keep a bald eagle feather you find lying on the ground unless you are Native American or Canadian Status Indian. Since eagle feathers have long been important to their cultures, tribal members may keep eagle feathers for religious and ceremonial purposes.

Look closely and you can see that this eagle has been banded. That means it has a small cuff on its ankle that helps researchers keep track of it and learn about the eagle's behavior in the wild.

Belted Kingfisher

Male

Female

These top-heavy fishing birds are quite a sight—and sound!—along Pacific Northwest rivers and streams.

SIZE: About the same size as a robin, belted kingfishers are about a foot long, but their head is much bigger. The most noticeable thing about them is their long, chunky beak.

COLOR & PATTERN: Belted kingfishers are bluish gray with a blue crest on their heads, a white collar, and a white belly. Unlike most other birds, kingfisher females are the ones with the added colorful stripe. You can spot the females by looking for their bright rust-colored belt.

SOUND: Belted kingfishers aren't songbirds, but you will always recognize their distinctive call after you hear it once. Their most common call is a high-pitched squeaky rattling sound.

NEST & EGGS: Belted kingfishers usually dig a burrow in the side of a bank near water. The burrow can go 3 to 6 feet into the bank, and both males and females take turns digging. They don't build a traditional nest inside, but instead lay five to eight glossy white eggs on the bare soil. The chicks hatch out with their eyes closed, helpless and naked.

FOOD: Listen for their squeaky, rattling cry, then watch a belted kingfisher swoop down to snag a fish for dinner. Don't look away once it has a catch! The bird may whack the fish against a tree branch to stun or kill it before swallowing it whole. Like an owl (see page 151), belted kingfishers regurgitate the parts of the fish they can't digest, so they don't bother sorting out what is and isn't edible when they eat.

REGION & HABITAT: Belted kingfishers are found all over North America and have even been spotted in Iceland. These big-headed, long-billed fish eaters are fun to observe near bodies of water throughout the Pacific Northwest. They won't visit your backyard feeder, so you'll want to go to a lake, pond, or river to watch kingfishers fishing.

SEASON: Belted kingfishers are year-round residents of the Pacific Northwest. In the colder parts of British Columbia, these birds will travel west or south for the coldest months of the year. If open water is available year-round, these birds may simply stay put.

Bewick's Wren

The scientific name for this bird family is Troglodytidae, which comes from the word *troglodyte*—meaning "cave dweller." Sometimes people use the word *troglodyte* to mean "like a caveman." Scientists picked this name because wrens like to forage for insects in crevices, or little caves. That can make them tricky to spot.

Wrens fall into the category of hard-to-identify little brown birds—or what birders call LBBs for short. How do you know if the little brown bird you're seeing is a wren? First, check out the tail. Does the bird hold its tail pointing straight up? If it does, that's probably a wren. Next, look at the bill. Wrens have a long, narrow, downward-pointed bill that's perfect for collecting insects and spiders on low shrubs. A lot of other LBBs have somewhat shorter and broader beaks that they use for crunching seeds.

There are at least six different species of wren in the Pacific Northwest. If it looks and acts like the species described below but has slightly different markings or seems to be in an odd place (like on a cactus or in a marsh), start your identification search by investigating other wrens in the area.

SIZE: Bewick's wrens can be up to around 5 inches long. They're small and quick, so don't look away, or you'll lose sight of this LBB.

COLOR & PATTERN: Bewick's wrens are brown and gray with lighter underparts and white eyebrows. Males and females look alike.

SOUND: Male Bewick's wrens sing, both to attract a mate and to ward off other wrens who might enter his territory. Each bird's song is just a little bit different than all the others' songs.

Who knew? Probably the most famous birder of all time was a man named John James Audubon. There's even a birding organization named after him: the National Audubon Society. Audubon studied and painted birds back in the 1800s, eventually creating a book called *The Birds of America*. He discovered and got to name many new species. The Bewick's wren (pronounced "Buicks," like the cars) was one such bird. Audubon named it after his friend Thomas Bewick, an Englishman who was interested in natural history.

NEST & EGGS: The male builds the nest out of sticks and other plant material inside a protective natural cavity. The female decides if she likes it. Sometimes the male builds several nests before the female chooses one that suits her. Then she'll move in and line the nest with soft feathers and animal hair. The female lays three to eight white eggs with reddish-brown spots per clutch and can have up to three clutches per season. Babies hatch out naked and helpless, weighing just a little more than a single birthday candle.

FOOD: Bewick's wrens are insectivores. They'll eat insects at every stage of development, including their eggs. While wrens usually forage at the edges of forests or bushes, these birds will sometimes come to backyard suet feeders as well.

REGION & HABITAT: Bewick's wrens live in the western part of the Pacific Northwest. To find them in British Columbia, go to the Vancouver area or Vancouver Island. These little birds like scraggly bushes and scrubland and can often be found in places with a combination of open space and larger plants for cover. They can sometimes even be seen in suburban gardens.

SEASON: Year-round.

Do you see a tiny wren—even smaller than the Bewick's—that looks kind of brown all over? You might be seeing a Pacific wren. (Good work! They can be hard to spot.) Your birder parents or grand-parents may still call this little bird a winter wren.

Pacific wren

But as ornithologists sometimes do, they changed the name back in 2010, when scientists decided it was really two different spe-cies: winter and Pacific wrens. The birds in our area are now called Pacific wrens, while "winter wren" is used to describe its look-alike on the East Coast.

Blackbird

Several species of birds are considered blackbirds. Three of the most common in the Pacific Northwest are the Brewer's blackbird, the brown-headed cowbird, and the red-winged blackbird. The males of all three species are mostly black, but not completely black from head to toe. That honor goes to crows and ravens, which you can read about on page 83.

Brewer's Blackbird

Male

Female

SIZE: Brewer's blackbirds are about the same size as a robin, around 8 to 10 inches long. The female is slightly smaller than the male.

COLOR & PATTERN: The scientists who named this bird were definitely looking at the male when they did it. Brewer's blackbird females are dull brown with dark eyes, and some have a metallic-greenish sheen on their backs. Males are glossy black all over and shine from bluish green to purple in the sunlight. The males also have yellow eyes, which makes them easy to pick out in a crowd.

SOUND: Brewer's blackbirds make a few different sounds. One is a "squee" that gets louder and higher at the end. Another is a repeating sound, like "chup, chup, chup."

NEST & EGGS: These blackbirds tend to nest up in trees near water in groups called colonies. The female builds a cup-shaped nest out of plant materials lined with soft grasses and hair. Sometimes she even adds a bit of mud or animal poop to act as cement. She will lay three to seven eggs per clutch and can sometimes have more than one clutch per year. The eggs are pale and spotted, and the chicks hatch out naked and helpless.

FOOD: These blackbirds love seeds, but they'll also eat insects, small animals, and even human trash.

REGION & HABITAT: Brewer's blackbirds can be found all over western North America in a wide variety of environments (including city streets). They naturally like scrublands, grasslands, and

"Hey, back off, birder!" This male Brewer's blackbird stands tall to protect the nearby females from threats.

meadows, but they've adapted well to human clearings such as golf courses, parks, and even parking lots.

SEASON: These birds live year-round in most of the Pacific Northwest. Blackbirds in central Canada migrate to the milder coast of British Columbia during the winter.

> Who knew? The Brewer's blackbird was first discovered by famous naturalist John James Audubon. This isn't the first bird he's named in this book. This time, Audubon named the blackbird after his friend and fellow ornithologist Thomas Brewer.

Brown-headed Cowbird

Male

Female

SIZE: Brown-headed cowbirds are about 8 inches long, the size of a small robin.

COLOR & PATTERN: Male brown-headed cowbirds are black with brown heads. Females and juveniles are a soft grayish brown all over and have dark, pointed beaks. Their feathers are lightest on their heads and underparts.

SOUND: Brown-headed cowbirds make a variety of whistles and chattering calls, and the males sing. Brown-headed cowbird babies are raised by foster bird parents (see page 63 for more on that), but they still learn to sing the songs and calls of the brown-headed cowbird instead of those sung by their foster families.

NEST & EGGS: Because brown-headed cowbirds rely on foster bird parents to raise their young, the mama brown-headed cowbird has more energy to lay eggs in a season than most birds—sometimes over thirty!

Brown-headed cowbirds are a type of bird known as a brood parasite. They use their neighbor birds as foster parents without their knowledge! Cowbirds lay their eggs in other birds' nests. The eggs hatch, and the big, hungry baby cowbirds usually win all the fights with the other babies in the nest for food. Their foster bird parents have no idea these fluffy giants aren't their own babies, and they work extra hard to keep them fed, often at the expense of their other babies. After they fledge (leave the nest), young cowbirds find a flock of other cowbirds to join. Check out these foster parents trying to feed their hungry brown-headed cowbird "offspring."

Her eggs are a little less than an inch long and are whitish with brown spots. Brown-headed cowbird babies hatch more quickly than other species, so they have an advantage over their younger foster brothers and sisters right from the start. Sometimes after a brown-headed cowbird hatches, it pushes the other eggs out of the nest.

Who knew? Scientists have discovered that after brown-headed cowbird babies fledge, they sneak off by themselves in the middle of the night to roost in an area around other brown-headed cowbirds. They return the next morning to be fed by their foster parents, though.

Brown-headed cowbird fledgling (left) and song sparrow foster parent (right)

FOOD: Brown-headed cowbirds got their name because they used to follow cattle and bison to eat the grasshoppers and other bugs kicked up as they wandered. They eat both seeds and insects.

One type of bird that doesn't have to worry about brown-headed cowbirds taking over their brood is the American goldfinch (see page 107). Unlike most other birds, goldfinches don't switch over to insects and other higher-protein food sources to feed their babies. Nestlings get the same food as their moms and dads: seeds. Brown-headed cowbird babies can't survive on that kind of diet, so these finches escape the cowbird baby hand-off.

REGION & HABITAT: Brown-headed cowbirds live all over most of North America at least part of the year. They like open, grassy areas like fields and meadows. They might also like your lawn, especially if there is bird-seed spilled on the ground under your feeder.

SEASON: You can see brown-headed cowbirds year-round along the West Coast and during the summer throughout most of the Pacific Northwest.

Red-winged Blackbird

Male

Female

SIZE: Red-winged blackbirds are about the same size as a robin (and a Brewer's blackbird), around 7 to 9 inches long.

COLOR & PATTERN: Here again, ornithologists named the bird after the male. Males are black all over and have red patches with bright yellow borders on their shoulders. They can flash those colors when they want to stand out, or they can tuck them away when they want to be less visible. The females aren't black or red at all, though. Instead, female red-winged blackbirds are brown streaked all over with a little yellow around their beaks and often a light-colored eyebrow. To identify a female, look at the shape of her body and pointy bill, and listen for the nearby male.

This juvenile male red-winged blackbird looks like a combination of his mom and dad. He's brown and stripy like a female, but he has the beginning of red arm bars like the male. You can also tell he's a juvenile by looking at the fluffy texture of the feathers on his body and head.

Who knew? The color schemes of the male and female red-winged blackbirds match their personalities. The male flies around calling "Look at me!" while the female flits through the low grasses trying to remain hidden. Her stripy brown feathers help her match the grasses, while her mate stands out against the sky to draw off predators. You can often see the males harassing local great blue herons to get the giant birds away from blackbird nests near the edge of a lake.

SOUND: The males have a song that sounds a little like "conk-la-lee." The female will answer back, "chit chit chit chit chit."

NEST & EGGS: Red-winged blackbirds like to make their nests near water. The female weaves a nest like a hammock, low among upright grasses. It hangs above the wet marsh, well hidden by the vegetation. She lays two to four pale eggs per clutch and can have more than one clutch per season. Chicks hatch out naked, blind, and helpless.

FOOD: That sharp beak tells you these birds love to eat insects. In fall and winter they also eat seeds, but give them a juicy green lacewing (insect) any day.

REGION & HABITAT: Red-winged blackbirds live all over North America. During breeding season (spring to summer), they prefer watery places like marshes. You can still see them there in the winter in the Pacific Northwest, but you might also see them feeding in

A red-winged blackbird with a green lacewing

huge flocks in open fields and grasslands. During breeding season, they're more territorial and solitary (they hang out alone or in pairs).

SEASON: In most of the Pacific Northwest (and the United States), you can see these birds year-round. In the colder parts of Canada, they migrate south and west (to the coast of British Columbia) for the winter.

Black-capped Chickadee

Chickadees fall into the "cute bird" category. They're round and fluffy with big dark eyes. There are several different species of chickadee in the Pacific Northwest, but the best known is probably the black-capped chickadee.

SIZE: Black-capped chickadees are small birds, averaging from around 4½ to almost 6 inches in length. They're fairly round without much of a neck, and their tail sticks out an inch or so past their back.

COLOR & PATTERN: Black-capped chickadees have light-colored underparts, tan on the sides fading to white on the belly. The bird's back is gray, and it has—as its name suggests—a black cap on its head with wide white stripes on its cheeks. They have a tiny black beak and round black eyes.

SOUND: The call of the black-capped chickadee sounds like "chick-a-dee-dee-dee!" Listen, and you'll understand where they got their name. Chickadees are one exception to the rule that songs are longer than calls. In this case, the song is just a few clear notes that some birders describe as sounding like "here sweetie!"

NEST & EGGS: All chickadees are cavity nesters, which means they build nests in small holes in trees and snags (dead trees). Sometimes they use old holes drilled out by woodpeckers, building a small nest inside from moss and twigs and lining it with soft animal fur. They're also a perfect candidate for a birdhouse hung in a safe spot in your yard. They especially like it when the inside is filled with sawdust or wood shavings they can dig out themselves. Make sure you put it up earlier than you think they'll need it, well before the breeding season in the spring. Once a chickadee chooses (or hollows out) a cavity, the female will build a soft nest inside. Her clutch can be as small as one or two tiny white eggs with reddish-brown spots, or as large as a dozen. Babies hatch almost completely naked with their eyes closed.

FOOD: Chickadees eat plants—including seeds, nuts, and berries—and bugs, including insects and spiders. They'll also come to a suet feeder for some nice, rich fat and will take sunflower seeds, nuts, and mealworms from standard feeders. If you look closely, you may even see a chickadee hanging upside down hunting bugs on a tree.

REGION & HABITAT: Black-capped chickadees can be found almost everywhere in the Pacific Northwest as well as across the northern United States and southern Canada. They are especially fond of deciduous forests (wooded areas mostly made up of trees with leaves that fall off seasonally).

Who knew? A lot of other species of birds hang out with chickadee flocks, especially if they're migrating through on their way to somewhere else. Scientists have discovered that even birds that don't have alarm calls of their own will alert to the chickadee's call of "chick-a-dee-dee-dee." And the more "dees" at the end of the call, the more serious the threat!

SEASON: Year-round.

A slightly smaller cousin of the black-capped chickadee that you might see around the Pacific Northwest is the chestnut-backed chickadee. Want to guess what color back it has? Chestnut is a reddish-brown color, and that brownish back is how you can tell this type of chickadee from all the others.

Chestnut-backed chickadee

Brown Creeper

Brown creepers are masters of camouflage—tiny little forest ninjas. They blend almost invisibly into their surroundings, so you have to look extra close to spot one even if it's right in front of you. Their spotted brown-and-beige back feathers are a perfect mimic of the tree bark where they spend their days hunting for small insects. Brown creepers are fairly common, but you might not ever see one if you don't slow down in the woods and give your eyes time to really look.

SIZE: Brown creepers are small birds, usually around 5 inches long. They appear kind of flat and wide from the back, which helps them disappear into the tree bark. If you look closely, you can see a brown creeper's feet sticking out on either side of its body helping it balance.

COLOR & PATTERN: These little birds look just like tree bark, with mottled (spotted or splotched) brown on their outer parts. Their underparts, which are usually up against the tree, are white.

SOUND: Brown creepers are hard to spot with your eyes, but you just might hear one singing if you're quiet. Their voices are high and delicate. Listen for the males singing. Birders often describe the song as sounding like "trees, beautiful trees!" Both males and females call to each other with high-pitched tweets.

NEST & EGGS: Brown creepers are so good at camouflage that their nests are really difficult to spot. They pick places where the bark has pulled away from the trunk of a tree and build a sort of hammock inside from little bits of things found nearby. The male helps collect the material, and the female builds the nest out of twigs, leaves, lichen, hair, feather, and even spider silk and cocoons. The female lays five to six eggs per clutch and has one clutch each year. Babies hatch pretty much naked except for a little fuzz on their heads.

FOOD: The brown creeper's slender, downward-curving bill is perfect for picking the small insects it loves to eat from tree bark. These birds can sometimes be lured to suet feeders in the winter (especially if other food is scarce), but you're most likely to see them hunting for bugs on big old trees.

REGION & HABITAT: These little tree creepers are found throughout the United States and much of Canada. Brown creepers live in forests with both deciduous trees (those that lose their leaves seasonally, typically in the fall) and evergreen trees (those that stay green all year).

SEASON: Brown creepers are found throughout most of North America at least part of the year. If you live in Canada, you might be more likely to see them in the summer, and if you live in the United States, you might see more in the winter. Here in the mature forests of the Pacific Northwest (all along the coast up through British Columbia and in the Rocky Mountains), you can find them year-round.

Who knew? Do you see a little bird that looks like a piece of tree bark creeping up the trunk of a large conifer? You might just be seeing a brown creeper. If you spot a similar-sized blue-gray bird moving *down* the tree, that's probably a nuthatch (see page 160). Brown creepers usually climb up and then fly back down to the base of the next tree to start over. Nuthatches usually do the opposite.

Bushtit

Male

Bushtits look like little mouse-birds, and you can watch them flit around bushes looking for tiny insects to eat. Sometimes whole shrubs can seem to come alive with bushtits, when flocks with as many as forty birds descend on the low trees and bushes (the understory) of a forest.

SIZE: These little birds are only about 3 inches long— the same size as some hummingbirds but much fluffier. They have rounded bodies and long, straight tails.

Female

COLOR & PATTERN: Bushtits have soft beige and gray feathers that help them blend quietly into the forest. Their exact color can vary by region, with West Coast birds having more brown on their heads than their inland cousins (which look gray). Mostly, they're just pale gray and tan, a little darker on their backs than on their bellies.

SOUND: Bushtits don't really sing a song, but they do chirp and tweet. That helps them keep track of each other while the flock spreads out to gather food. If there's a threat or an intruder in their area, they can let each other know quickly.

NEST & EGGS: A bushtit nest looks a lot like an old gym sock hanging from a tree—if your old gym socks were woven out of moss, spider webs, tree pieces, and lichen. It hangs down about a foot long from where it connects to the branch, and there is a small opening at the top for the birds to use as a door. You can spot these nests anywhere from just a few feet off the ground to a hundred feet in the air. You're most likely to get a good look at one hanging near a path or other open area.

Male and female bushtits build their nests together. Once a clutch of eggs has been laid (between four and ten little white eggs per clutch), bushtits often have extra adult helpers—usually males—around to help them care for the nest and babies. This is really uncommon in the bird world. All of the adults and babies sleep together in the nest while it is in use. Also, bushtits reuse their nests for a second clutch in a season if they can. (Good thing, because those nests can take a whole month to build!)

FOOD: Bushtits are gleaners—a type of insect eater that picks the tiniest bugs off of plants. They flit quickly through the branches, hunting tiny

bugs to eat. You can watch them in your yard, too, if you put out a suet feeder (especially in winter). The great thing about feeding bushtits with suet feeders is that when one comes, he brings all his friends!

REGION & HABITAT: Bushtits can be found in most of the western United States and down into Mexico, but if you want to see them in Canada, head for Vancouver Island or Vancouver, BC. Bushtits like low bushes and small trees. They can be easy to miss in a forest, but you can also spot them in parks, yards, and near ponds and streams. If you stare patiently at a bush and spy some movement, that might well be a bushtit.

SEASON: Year-round.

Who knew? Unlike many birds, it's easy to tell male and female bushtits apart just by looking at their eyes. The females have a pale circle around their pupil that makes them look kind of wild-eyed. The males have solid dark eyes like a mouse. Look at this photo. *Can you spot the female?*

California Quail

Male (left) and female (right)

California quail are truly one of the funniest birds to watch. They can fly short distances, but they often choose to run instead when they're frightened. They look so silly running bellies-first with their wings stuck to their sides!

Both the male and the female have a dangly topknot on their head. It looks like a single feather, but it's actually made up of six overlapping feathers. The male's topknot is bigger and more noticeable than the female's. While the female pecks around on the ground for food, the male will often find a good spot to stand watch.

SIZE: California quail are medium-sized, bigger than a robin. They're usually around 10 inches long, and they're chubby for a bird.

COLOR & PATTERN: Males are gray and brown with a black-and-white mask on their face. Females are more delicate-looking, softer gray and beige with no mask.

SOUND: Some people describe the California quail's call as "Chi-ca-go" (like the city) but like most bird calls, that's a little bit of a stretch. It sounds more like if you sang "Chi-ca-go" into a kazoo.

NEST & EGGS: California quail usually nest on the ground hidden in grasses or bushes. The female lines a shallow depression on the ground with grass or twigs. She lays more than a dozen eggs per clutch. Each egg is a little over an inch long and is white or cream colored with brown flecks. As soon as they hatch, the babies can walk around with their parents pecking for food.

FOOD: California quail's first choice of food is seeds and grain. They won't turn down a tasty grub now and then, though.

REGION & HABITAT: These birds have California in their names, but they also live in Oregon, Washington, Idaho, and parts of southern British Columbia. California quail are skittish, but they're often found near people anyway. They like our yards and parks and farms. Quail need a combination of some kind of cover for protection (grass, brush, trees) and more open ground where they can scratch for food. If you want to

These juvenile quail aren't that much smaller than their parents, but their round fluffiness and softer coloring let birders know they aren't fully grown yet.

feed them in your yard, you'll need to put birdseed out on the ground.
They're also pretty happy cleaning up under feeders where other birds
or squirrels have spilled seed below.

SEASON: Year-round.

> Who knew? After babies hatch, several pairs of quail may mix
> together and raise all the little ones together. A group of quail is called
> a covey. Some coveys have more than seventy-five birds in them!

Cedar Waxwing

Cedar waxwings almost look like they are carved out of wood. Their peach-and-gray bodies and elegant crests make this a lovely bird to find in the Pacific Northwest.

SIZE: Cedar waxwings are a little smaller than a robin, averaging between 5½ and 6½ inches.

COLOR & PATTERN: Their peachy-brown head and chest blend down into a light yellow belly. The wings and back are gray, and the tips of the tail are bright yellow. They have a noticeable crest of feathers on their head and a black mask with a white rim across their eyes. Many also have bright red waxy tips on their middle wing feathers. Waxwings actually have wax on their wings!

Who knew? While scientists aren't really sure why cedar waxwings have waxy red wingtips—some think it has to do with their diet—they have noticed something interesting. If you count the red tips on a waxwing's feathers, you can get a sense of its age. If it's immature, it will have fewer than five red tips per wing. If it's older, it can have more than nine.

SOUND: While cedar waxwings don't sing songs, they do call to each other. Their calls are kind of high-pitched and buzzy sounding, like an insect.

NEST & EGGS: These birds often nest near other cedar waxwings up in the fork of a tree branch. Each female builds a cup-shaped nest out of grass, twigs, and other materials, sometimes even stealing bits from other birds' nests. She lays two to six pale blue-gray (sometimes spotted) eggs per clutch and can have more than one clutch per season. Babies hatch out naked, helpless, and about the same weight as three medium paper clips.

FOOD: These birds love fruit, especially small berries and cherries. In the winter, they like to dine on cedar berries, which explains

the first part of their name. If you have fruit trees around your neighborhood, you may also have cedar waxwings visiting your yard. They'll also eat an occasional insect for variety. Cedar waxwings swallow the seeds of the fruit they eat whole and then poop them out later. Because of this, they are a great method of seed dispersal (how seeds get spread around) for fruit-bearing plants.

Who knew? Sometimes cedar waxwings eat fruit that's overripe or just not good for them. They can become "drunk" or even die from the alcohol produced by the rotting fruit. Some landscaping plants (such as nandina, a common shrub with small red berries) can be especially toxic. If you have those growing in your yard and want to be sure the birds are safe, either trim away and discard the berries or make sure there are plenty of better food options for the birds to choose.

Nandina

REGION & HABITAT: Cedar waxwings are common throughout North America. They live in flocks anywhere there is fruit. Look for them around trees, shrubs, and low plants that bear fruit or berries, often near water.

SEASON: Cedar waxwings are around all year in most of the Pacific Northwest. As you move north into Canada, they become spring and summer visitors.

Crow and Raven

Crow

Crows and ravens both belong to a group of birds called corvids. (Jays are in that group too. You can learn more about jays on page 176.) Corvids are some of the smartest birds out there. Scientists have discovered that they can do high-level tasks like solving puzzles, using tools, playing games, mimicking other animals (including humans), and recognizing faces.

There are several species of both crows and ravens, but in the Pacific Northwest you're most likely to see the American crow and the common raven.

Raven

Crows and ravens are both all black, which makes it easy to confuse the two. But if you look and listen carefully, you can see and hear the differences. The two most visible differences are the body and beak size.

SIZE: American crows are usually between 16 and 20 inches long—quite a bit bigger than a robin—with a wingspan around 3 feet.

Common ravens are bigger than American crows—usually between 22 and 27 inches long with a wingspan of almost 4 feet. When you look at their entire body size (not just the length, but the width and weight too), ravens are about twice as big overall as crows. Another difference is that ravens' beaks are much bigger compared to the size of their heads. Raven beaks are noticeably huge and sort of bent on top. You can also usually see more long, shaggy feathers called hackles on the raven's throat.

Crow

COLOR & PATTERN: Crows and ravens are the only all-black birds in North America. Even their brown eyes are so dark they look black from a distance. All other "blackbirds" have some other color somewhere—on their beaks, legs, or feathers. You can tell baby crows and ravens from the adults by their blue eyes and less shiny feathers. As they get a little older, juveniles' eyes turn caramel brown and then nearly black by the time they're adults.

Raven

SOUND: American crows make a "caw!" call that is familiar to most people. Often, birders find large raptors such as owls by listening for the loud squawks and caws of nearby crows. Crows (and many other birds) will "mob," or gang up on, larger birds to protect their territory.

Common ravens make many different sounds, but the most often heard is a deep croak. A raven can also make a loud clicking noise by clacking its beak together.

NEST & EGGS: Both crows and ravens nest up high. In addition to the tops of tall trees, they sometimes build nests on cliffs or on tall human-made structures like bridges and utility poles.

Have you ever heard of a "crow's nest" on a ship? That's what sailors call the lookout platform on the very top of the main mast. It's way up there like an actual crow's nest at the top of a tree.

Crow couples build their nests together out of sticks and twigs. The size of the nest can range from as small as 6 inches to as large as a foot and a half across. The eggs are pale blue-green, and the babies hatch out naked except for little tufts of gray down. Offspring often stay around their parents for the first couple of years and help care for future broods.

Raven nests are mostly built by the females out of large sticks. The nests can be as big as 5 feet across on the outside. The eggs are usually

Fledgling crow

greenish and spotted and are about 2 inches long. Like crows, the babies hatch out naked and helpless.

Both crows and ravens mate for life. When they choose a partner, they will interact with soft coos, and they'll nuzzle each other's faces, preening each other and touching beaks.

Crow

FOOD: Crows and ravens are both omnivores, which means they'll eat both plants and animals. Actually, they'll eat pretty much anything they can find, including other birds' eggs, berries, small animals, nuts, carrion, pet food, and garbage. The main difference between the diets of American crows and common ravens is that crows eat more garbage, and ravens eat more carrion.

REGION & HABITAT: Both crows and ravens are widespread through-out the United States and Canada. They are smart and adaptable (they can change their behavior to fit new circumstances), so they can live wherever they can find food and shelter. Crows like open areas with a few trees or buildings to perch in. You're much more likely to spot them in a city than in the deep woods. Ravens also live around cities, but they prefer wilder areas like the Pacific coast because they rely more on carrion for their diet.

Raven

Who knew? Crows band together in a flock called a murder. Have you ever seen a murder of crows? While most big groups of birds are just called flocks, many birders like to use and laugh at this funny group name. Crows are so social that they even have "funerals" when one of their flock dies. They gather in large groups and pay their respects to the dead.

In some cities, the flocks of crows have gotten so huge that they're becoming a problem for the people trying to live and work there. In Portland, Oregon, officials have tried something from nature to discourage the flocks of up to 15,000 crows from roosting in town.

A trained hawk from Integrated Avian Solutions

They've hired falconers (people who train and work with raptors) to bring in hawks to scare off the crows. The hawks are well fed and trained, and they don't hunt the crows for food. They just harass the crows enough so they want to move on to find a new place to sleep.

SEASON: Both crows and ravens live year-round in most of the Pacific Northwest, and during the summer up in western British Columbia. In the fall and winter, crows come together into massive roosting flocks that can have tens of thousands of birds.

See the hackles at the raven's throat?

Who knew? It's sometimes easiest to tell crows and ravens apart when they're flying. Crows have a laid-back flapping style, but they rarely ever soar. They fly straight to where they're trying to go. The old expression "as the crow flies" refers to the crow's tendency to fly in a straight line to where it's going. Ravens like to soar like a hawk or an eagle does, and sometimes they even do rolls or other tricks in the air. If you can see the tail feathers, there's a tell-tale difference there too. Crow tails are flat across the back. All the tail feathers are the same length. Raven tail feathers are longer in the middle and shorter on the sides, so their tails are sort of pointed like a shovel.

American crow tail

Common raven tail

Fan-shaped

Wedge-shaped

Dark-eyed Junco

Male

Female

These sweet little birds are common here in the Pacific Northwest. Look for them hopping around on the ground looking for food—especially under feeders.

SIZE: Dark-eyed juncos are small birds about 5½ to a little over 6 inches long.

COLOR & PATTERN: While all dark-eyed juncos look similar, their exact colors can range dramatically depending on where you spot them. You could line them up and they'd look like a bunch of different birds if you just looked at the color. Dark-eyed juncos on the East Coast are more grayish, while the juncos here in the Pacific Northwest are more brownish. The type we see in the West is sometimes called the Oregon junco, but they're still part of the dark-eyed junco species. (They used to be their own species, but ornithologists like to keep us on our toes.) Male dark-eyed juncos in the Pacific Northwest have a dark brown or gray-to-black head and a

reddish-brown back. Their sides often show a soft peachy color. Females look like a softer version of the males. Their heads are lighter, but you can still see a darker cap that looks like a hood. The junco's beak is light and somewhat pinkish. The eyes (as the name suggests) are black. All dark-eyed juncos have white feathers on both sides of their tail. When they flush (take off flying), junco tails flash open like a section of an umbrella, alternating white-black-white out from the center. This is a great way to identify a dark-eyed junco that you've startled off of a trail.

SOUND: The dark-eyed junco's song is a trilling sound—a long stream of the same notes made in rapid succession.

This juvenile dark-eyed junco can be a tricky bird to identify. It's missing the distinct hood of its parents. It doesn't have those soft-colored underparts. It even has stripes! *How on earth can you tell it's a junco?* Well, first of all, in spring and summer, when this  photo was taken, striped or speckled feathers often mean a bird is a juvenile, so ignore that for now. Check out that beak! It's definitely a seed eater with that strong triangular shape. And it's pink! There aren't a lot of little birds with a pink seed-eating beak. Guess who has one? A dark-eyed junco! Learning to look for less obvious details like these can help you identify all kinds of juveniles.

NEST & EGGS: Dark-eyed juncos usually nest on the ground, but occasionally they'll pick a spot such as a hanging flower basket. If one takes up residence in a flowerpot at your house, be careful of the birds and eggs when you water your plant. Do your best to keep the nest and its residents as undisturbed (and dry) as possible. The female lays three to six small whitish (with tinges of blue or green) eggs speckled with brown and green. She can have up to three broods per season. Babies hatch out mostly naked and helpless.

FOOD: Juncos eat mostly seeds, but they also eat the occasional insect or spider, especially during the breeding season. A lot of birds switch their diets from seeds to higher-protein insects when they have babies to feed.

REGION & HABITAT: Dark-eyed juncos are some of the most common birds in North America. They thrive all over the continent, from down in Mexico to all the way up in Alaska. You'll find dark-eyed juncos in backyards, parks, and woods throughout the Pacific Northwest. They like to eat on the ground, so if you have feeders, look for them underneath, snacking on the seeds other birds have dropped.

SEASON: In some places dark-eyed juncos are called snowbirds because they show up in the wintertime when other birds have migrated south. Here in the Pacific Northwest we are lucky enough to have these little songbirds all year long. This is a great species to watch in the winter too, because they fluff up their downy feathers to stay warm and end up looking like little round puffballs.

Duck

A duck is one of the birds many kids learn to identify first. But it really isn't one kind of bird at all. It's many different species that all have a few basic things in common. Ducks are waterfowl, part of a larger family that also includes geese and swans. They are found in every part of the world except Antarctica. In the Pacific Northwest you can often find ducks anywhere there's water.

What makes a duck a duck? Well, those webbed feet, for starters. Ducks also have a flat bill that works well for straining pond water for tasty things to eat. Their feathers are designed to keep their inner downy layer dry even when they dive or *duck* underwater. And finally, the male and female bird of most types of ducks have very different looks. The male is usually brighter and more colorful than the female, especially during mating season. Male ducks are called drakes, and females are called hens or just plain ducks.

There are so many different types of ducks in the Pacific Northwest that they could easily have their own book. Here are a few that you might see in ponds and lakes near you. When you go looking, be ready to jot down notes on others you spot to add to your life list.

Hooded Merganser

Male

Female

SIZE: Hooded mergansers are the smallest of the three ducks profiled in this book. They range from just under 16 inches to just over 19 inches long.

COLOR & PATTERN: The hooded merganser gets its name from the feathered hood on the heads of both the male and the female. They're different colors: The male's hood is black and white to go with his sharply striped black, white, and chestnut-brown body. The female's hood is brown like the rest of her. The hoods can lie flat when the mergansers are just hanging out, but when they want to show off for each other, poof! Those hoods puff right up.

SOUND: Hooded mergansers don't make much sound at all. They like to float in silence. When they do call—like when they're trying to find a mate or keep track of new hatchlings—their calls range from a deep, throaty croak, like a frog, to various whistles. When the female flies, she sometimes makes a sound like "croo crook!"

NEST & EGGS: Hooded mergansers are cavity nesters. After the female builds the nest, she pulls feathers from her breast to line it and help keep the eggs warm. That adds insulation for the babies and makes it easier for the heat from the mama's body to pass on to the eggs. If she can't find a cavity or nesting box that suits her, a female hooded merganser might just lay her eggs in another female's nest. Like brown-headed cowbirds, this makes them brood parasites (discussed on page 63). But ducks usually only lay their eggs in the

These two males are showing off a courting move called head-throwing, where they throw their heads back with their hoods raised to try to get the female's attention.

nests of their own species. They lay up to a dozen eggs per clutch, but some mamas have found themselves with more than forty eggs because of all the other female mergansers dropping off their extras. Ducklings (baby ducks) of all species are fluffy, alert, and ready to leave the nest with their parents soon after hatching.

FOOD: Hooded mergansers are fun to watch as they feed because they dive down under the water to catch their prey. (See a photo on page 24.) They love to snack on crayfish and other shallow-water animals, as well as small fish. It's amazing to see what big critters these little ducks can swallow.

REGION & HABITAT: Hooded mergansers can be found throughout the Pacific Northwest and across the United States and Canada near forested wetlands, ponds, and small lakes.

SEASON: These small ducks can be found year-round along the Pacific Northwest coast as well as further inland in British Columbia and Washington State. In the rest of the Northwest, hooded mergansers migrate and can be spotted in the wintertime and during migration in the fall.

Mallard

Male

Female

SIZE: Mallards are fairly large birds. They vary from around 20 to 25 inches long.

COLOR & PATTERN: Mallards are the ducks you're most likely to see swimming in a local pond. The females are mottled brown with an orange-and-brown bill, while the males are more brightly colored. They have bright yellow beaks and iridescent green heads. When feathers are iridescent, it means they shine with different colors when the light hits them. Their bodies are brown, gray, and black. Both the male and female have a little patch of bright blue on both wings.

SOUND: When you imagine a duck quacking, you're probably thinking of the sound of a female mallard.

They often quack many times in a row. The male makes more of a raspy call only a couple of times in a row.

NEST & EGGS: Mallards are ground nesters. They'll choose a dry spot near the water and will scrape out a shallow bowl in the ground. The female lines her nest with nearby grasses and leaves. As with other ducks, the female mallard will also add her own down feathers to keep the eggs and babies warm. She might lay anywhere from one to over a dozen eggs in a single clutch. They look a lot like the chicken eggs you see at the grocery store.

FOOD: Mallards are dabbling ducks. Dabbling ducks feed in two ways. One is by skimming for floating plants and critters on the surface of the water. The other, called dabbling, is by tipping their bodies down in the water to dig through the mud at the bottom of the pond. While they dig for underwater plants, insects, and other tasty snacks, their back ends point straight up!

REGION & HABITAT: The mallard is the most common waterbird in North America. If you go to a local pond, lake, or river, you have a great chance of spotting these ducks.

SEASON: Year-round.

Wood Duck

Male

Female

SIZE: Wood ducks are a little smaller than mallards. They range from around 18 to 21 inches long.

COLOR & PATTERN: Wood ducks are some of the prettiest waterfowl in the Pacific Northwest. The males have iridescent green heads with striking white outlining, a rusty-brown chest, and tan sides. The feathers on their heads shift from green to purple in the sunlight. They also have blue, black, yellow, and red accents on their feathers, eyes, and bill. The females are softer toned but still lovely. The pale colors on their wings almost look like stained glass or a kaleidoscope.

SOUND: Male and female wood ducks sound different from each other, and nothing at all like mallards. Female wood ducks make a call that birders describe as sounding like "ooo-eek!" The males have a whistling kind of chirp. The truth is, not all ducks say "quack"!

NEST & EGGS: Wood ducks nest in tree cavities—sometimes as far up as 50 to 60 feet off the ground. Duck-sized cavities can be hard to find, though, so wood ducks will happily use nesting boxes nailed to waterside trees. Like other ducks, a female wood duck will line her nest with feathers pulled from her own breast. Like hooded mergansers, wood ducks sometimes lay their eggs in another female's nest. Wood ducks can lay up to sixteen eggs per clutch. Babies hatch out alert and covered with down. They're ready to explore with their parents the very next day.

FOOD: Wood ducks, like all ducks, are omnivores, so they eat a lot of different kinds of food. In the wild they eat proteins such as fish, insects, slugs, crawdads, frogs, and lamprey. They also enjoy grass, leaves, algae, seeds, fruit, and grain. You know what isn't great for ducks, though? Bread. And if they don't eat it and it goes in the water, it also messes up their home. If you want to feed ducks, be sure to check with the experts nearby to find out what types of foods would be best for the birds. Some parks encourage duck fans to offer cracked corn, oats, or even lettuce leaves instead of bread.

Wood duck male (left) and female (right) resting on a log

REGION & HABITAT: Wood ducks can be found across the United States and parts of Canada. They live in most of the Pacific Northwest, but if you want to see them in British Columbia, head to areas near the US border, like Vancouver, BC, and Vancouver Island. They are happiest when they can have water as well as plant and tree cover. You're likely to see these ducks in streams with trees growing nearby. They also like beaver ponds, marshes, and swamps.

SEASON: Wood ducks can be seen year-round in most of the Northwest, and they're around during the summer up in British Columbia.

Falcon

Falcons are small to medium-sized raptors that hunt during the day. Two of the most commonly seen falcons in the Pacific Northwest are the American kestrel and the peregrine falcon.

American Kestrel

Male

Female

SIZE: Kestrels are the smallest falcons in North America—cute but still fierce. They're a little bigger than a robin, averaging around 9 to 12 inches long.

COLOR & PATTERN: Kestrels are colorful, common, and fairly easy to spot if you know what to look for. Both males and females have warm reddish-brown backs and pale bellies with black spots over everything. The males have grayish-blue wings, while the females have brown wings. Kestrels all have a black band near the end of their squared-off tail. Both males and females have two vertical black stripes on each cheek. Some birders call these the mustache and the sideburn.

SOUND: American kestrels make a loud, shrill call that sounds like "klee klee klee!"

NEST & EGGS: Kestrels are cavity nesters that use holes they find in old trees and even in human structures. They don't drill out their own holes or even move in any nesting material. Kestrels take what they can find. The female lays four to five eggs per clutch. The eggs are white to light yellow and spotted with purple or brown. Baby kestrels hatch out helpless, with their pink skin showing through patchy white down.

FOOD: These falcons eat small rodents, large insects, snakes, frogs, and occasionally small birds.

Who knew? Raptors are known for their great eyesight, but some—kestrels included—have a next-level adaptation for hunting. They can see ultraviolet light. That's a type of light beyond the violet side of the rainbow that humans can't see. This helps kestrels hunt since mice and other small mammals mark their trails with urine (pee), which reflects ultraviolet light. They can see mouse pee trails!

REGION & HABITAT: American kestrels live all over North and South America. They like open grasslands and meadows where they can easily hunt. They do well around people because they can take advantage of human-created flatlands like parks and farms. You can spot them sitting on utility wires or poles looking out over fields for their prey. They often pump their tail up and down as they watch and wait.

SEASON: American kestrels are year-round residents in most of the Pacific Northwest. They can be found inland in Canada during the summer months.

Peregrine Falcon

So fast it can hunt down other birds in flight, the peregrine falcon is a favorite of birders all over the world. They've been trained for thousands of years by humans called falconers to help in their own hunts.

SIZE: These fierce bird-eating falcons are about the size of a crow, ranging from around 14 to 19 inches long. Male and female peregrine falcons look the same unless you see them side by side. Like many raptors, the female peregrine is larger than the male.

COLOR & PATTERN: These birds are dark bluish gray on top and white underneath with dark horizontal markings called barring on their bellies. They have yellow legs, and their beaks are yellow with a black curved tip.

SOUND: Peregrine falcons don't make a lot of noise, but you might hear their warning call that sounds like "kack, kack, kack, kack, kack."

NEST & EGGS: Peregrine falcons like to nest on rocky cliffs. They don't build an actual nest, but they'll scrape off a little area on the cliff before the female lays her eggs. She will lay from two to five eggs once per season. The eggs are about the size of a chicken egg, but they can be brownish and spotted. Babies hatch out helpless, covered in fuzzy white down, and weighing about as much as half of a peanut butter sandwich.

FOOD: Peregrine falcons usually eat other birds, and they're perfectly adapted for the hunt. These raptors can dive at speeds over 200 miles per hour while chasing prey, which makes the peregrine falcon the fastest animal on Earth. And not only are they fast, but they pack quite a punch! At the end of that super-fast dive, the peregrine falcon clenches its feet into fists and smashes them into its prey, knocking it out.

REGION & HABITAT: Peregrine falcons are one of the most common raptors worldwide. They can be found on every continent except Antarctica. Your best chance of spotting this falcon in the Pacific Northwest is along the Pacific coast, but you can find them inland too. Look for them anywhere there are cliffs that they can use for nesting. Also, because they've decided skyscrapers and bridges make decent substitute cliffs, peregrine falcons are one of the birds that has adapted well to living near or in cities.

SEASON: You can find peregrine falcons along the Pacific Northwest coast any time of year and inland during migration times in the fall and spring. The word *peregrine* actually means "wanderer," named after the birds' migration.

> **Who knew?** Along with bald eagles, peregrine falcons were almost completely wiped out in the United States back in the middle part of the twentieth century. One major problem was a pesticide called DDT. Scientists created DDT to get rid of insects on crops. They didn't realize those chemicals would also hurt the birds until it was almost too late. The United States stopped using DDT in the 1970s (Canada stopped in the 1980s), and the eagles and peregrine falcons have made an amazing comeback.

Finch

Finches include many different species of small to medium-sized (and sometimes brightly colored) songbirds, all with the same basic shape and similar behaviors. It's not uncommon to find more than one kind of finch flocking together. (They love a crowd.)

A few of the most common Pacific Northwest finches are described in the following pages.

Male American goldfinch in summer plumage

Female American goldfinch in summer plumage

American Goldfinch

SIZE: American goldfinches are small birds, averaging between 4 and 5½ inches long.

COLOR & PATTERN: Male and female American goldfinches are known for having bright yellow bodies with black accents, including black wings on both sexes and a black top to the male's head. Both males and females have a white bar across their black wings. These finches molt twice a year, which allows them to put on a bright yellow-and-black outfit for the summer mating season and a duller brownish look for the winter. Starting in September, American

Male American goldfinch changing over from winter to summer plumage

American goldfinch in winter plumage

goldfinches start to replace their feathers with duller colors, turning mostly light brown and black. Even their beaks get duller and darker! After molting for about eight weeks, they will be wearing their off-season (winter) plumage (feathers). They start to change back to yellow in February or March and are back to their full breeding plumage by May. No matter what season it is, female American goldfinches are less brightly colored than the males. In the dead of winter, though, it can be hard to tell the males and females apart.

SOUND: Male goldfinches have a long, twittering song that they use to impress the females. The most common sound they make, though, is their contact call. That's the sound birds make while they're flying or feeding to keep track of other members of their flock. Some birders say it sounds like "po-ta-to-chip." That may be a stretch. But if you hear a burst of four tweets that sound like they follow the rhythm of "potato chip," that could very well be an American goldfinch.

NEST & EGGS: Female goldfinches build cup-shaped nests in shrubs or small trees out of thin rootlets, stems, twigs, and other plant material. They line their nests with the down from the thistles they eat for food. Goldfinches wait until late summer to lay their eggs when the thistle plants bloom, which is well after most birds have already had their first set of chicks. That means the seeds they love to eat will be ready when their babies are born. Female American goldfinches will lay

Male American goldfinch baby

between two and seven pale blue (almost white), sometimes spotted eggs per clutch.

FOOD: Finches have the perfect cone-shaped beak for cracking their diet of mostly seeds. If you want to attract them to your yard, seed feeders are your best bet, especially filled with black sunflower seeds and/or nyjer seeds.

REGION & HABITAT: The American goldfinch lives all over North America at least part of the year and is the state bird of Washington. They like open scrubland and fields. Finches do fairly well in and around human developments (yards, farms, parks, etc.). You will often see large flocks of goldfinches in suburban neighborhoods.

SEASON: American goldfinches can be found year-round in much of the Pacific Northwest, though some Canadian flocks do migrate south as it gets colder. Look for the bright yellow finches in the summertime, and remember that they'll look more brown than yellow in the winter.

House Finch

Male

Female

SIZE: House finches are small birds, averaging between 5 and 5½ inches long.

COLOR & PATTERN: House finch males and females both have gray seed-eating beaks and streaky gray-brown bodies and tails, but the male usually has a bright red head. His head could also be orange or even yellow instead, depending on his diet. Female and juvenile house finches are examples of what birders call little brown birds (LBBs) or little brown jobs (LBJs). Even though they're common, identifying them can be a challenge. Look for streaked feathers and the cone shape of the bill, and see if you can spot a nearby male.

SOUND: Male house finches have a long twittering song that has made them popular with people who keep birds as caged pets. Males and females also make a sharp cheeping call.

NEST & EGGS: House finches usually build cup-shaped nests in trees or on human structures. The nest is built out of thin rootlets (small roots), stems, twigs, and other plant material. Females can lay between two and six eggs per clutch and can have up to a whopping six clutches per season. Since all finches (and lots of other birds) can have more than one clutch per year, be sure to leave their nests alone even if you see that the babies have left the nest.

FOOD: House finches eat mostly seeds and also flower buds and fruit.

REGION & HABITAT: House finches originally lived throughout western North America. Back in 1940, people captured them to sell as pets in New York, and some ended up being released into the wild. Now house finches are common all over the eastern United States too. That tends to happen when people bring birds, plants, and animals to places where they aren't native. In the Pacific Northwest, they live in many different types of habitats: grasslands, deciduous forests, deserts, and streamsides. You can find them most easily where there are humans, around manmade lawns and buildings.

SEASON: House finches can be found throughout much of the Pacific Northwest year-round.

If you see a finch with a wash of pink or redness over his whole body, that's probably not a house finch at all. Instead, it's a close look-alike called a purple finch. (No, they're not actually purple. Go figure.)

Learn about another kind of finch—the grosbeak—on page 120.

Purple finch

Goose

There are several different species of geese that live in the Pacific Northwest.

One of the most common, the Canada goose, has at least eleven subspecies with slight differences in appearance, color, and size. That's a lot of just slightly different-looking geese for one species! It's great just to look at the main characteristics for this one as a beginning birder.

Snow geese, another species you can see in the Pacific Northwest, are a migrating visitor. These big white birds are best known for their giant, noisy traveling flocks.

Geese are big, confident, and protective birds. If you choose not to respect their space, they may fly at you with loud honks and even a nip or two. They're great to admire from a distance, but never *ever* get on the bad side of a goose.

Canada Goose

SIZE: Canada geese are large, up to about 43 inches tall, and they're fairly heavy for a bird. A Canada goose can weigh in at over 19 pounds!

COLOR & PATTERN: Canada geese have a black head and neck with a wide white strap

that goes under their chin and up both cheeks. The rest of their body is tan and brown. Goslings (baby geese) start out fluffy and yellow, and gradually start looking more and more like their parents over the course of their first year.

SOUND: Geese are best known for their loud honking call. You can hear many of them calling together when a flock of geese takes off or lands nearby.

NEST & EGGS: Canada geese are waterfowl who make their nests on the ground out of dried grass, moss, lichen, and their own downy feathers. The mama lays from two to eight creamy white eggs per clutch, and each egg is over 3 inches long. That's a big egg, but baby geese are pretty big too. The goslings can leave the nest to follow their parents after only a day or two. Young geese stay with their parents for pretty much a whole year, which is unusually long for a bird.

Who knew? Canada geese mate for life. And when picking a partner, they tend to pick a goose close to their own size. That means small geese partner with small geese, and large geese partner with large geese. In each pair, the male is usually a little bigger than the female.

FOOD: Geese are herbivores (plant eaters). They enjoy grasses, seeds, grains, and aquatic plants. If you look around where geese have been eating, you can see their grassy green droppings, sometimes as big as a small dog's.

REGION & HABITAT: Canada geese live all over North America, from Canada down to parts of Mexico. They are often found in large flocks and are especially fond of big lawns in places like neighborhood parks and golf courses. You can even see them in mowed patches of grass along the freeway. Some scientists think they like short grass both because they can eat it and because they can see predators coming from far off.

SEASON: Even though Canada geese are migrating birds, we can see them all year in most of the Pacific Northwest. Birders who live inland in British Columbia or in parts of central Washington will have the best luck looking for them in the summer and early fall. When you look up in the sky, you'll likely see the classic V-shaped formation of geese flying south for the winter.

Who knew? Sometimes broods of goslings from different families will mix together in big groups with one or more adults. These "gang broods" look a lot like a class of grade-school kids!

Snow Goose

SIZE: Snow geese are a little smaller than Canada geese but still big for a bird. They're usually between 27 and 33 inches long, and their wingspan is around 54 inches.

COLOR & PATTERN: Snow geese have white bodies and heads, and their wing tips are black (you can see that best when they're flying). Their legs and bill are both pink. If you look closely, you might notice a dark line between the upper and lower beak. That line is called the grinning patch. (Does the goose look like it's smiling?) Sometimes you may also see a snow goose with a dark gray body (but still a white head) mixed in with the others. That's a snow goose, but it's a less common variety called a blue goose.

SOUND: These are some of the noisiest birds in the Pacific Northwest, especially when they're in a huge flock. The honking sounds coming off a marsh where they've settled can be ear-splitting.

NEST & EGGS: The female scrapes a shallow hollow in dry ground and may start actually laying eggs before adding in nesting materials such as sea grass and seaweed, along with feathers she plucks from her breast to keep the eggs warm. She lays two to six big white eggs, and the babies hatch out ready to leave the nest almost immediately.

FOOD: Snow geese are herbivores, and they love snacking on grasses and other plants—any part of the plants they can get their beaks on. These birds have huge appetites! Sometimes that can be a problem for farmers.

REGION & HABITAT: Snow geese migrate over large swaths of North America, but they only breed in a few places in the far north—places like northern Canada and Alaska, Greenland, and even Siberia. Here in the Pacific Northwest you can find them resting and filling their bellies in fields, marshes, wetlands, and on shallow lakes.

SEASON: We're most likely to see snow geese in the Pacific Northwest during their fall and spring migrations. They fly overhead in huge flocks of sometimes more than 50,000 birds.

Great Blue Heron

If you've spent any time near a lake, river, or saltwater shore in the Pacific Northwest, you've probably seen a great blue heron. These stately birds are often staring into the water, motionlessly searching for their next meal. Looking at one, it's easy to see why scientists now say birds are descended from dinosaurs.

SIZE: Great blue herons are one of the largest birds in the Pacific Northwest. They can stand over 4 feet tall and have over a 6-foot wingspan.

Who knew? Think of someone who is the same size as a heron, about 4 feet tall. How much does she weigh? Can you pick her up easily? Great blue herons are a great example of just how much lighter bird bodies are than our own. That 4-foot tall heron weighs no more than 5½ pounds. That's just a little more than a full gallon of milk!

COLOR & PATTERN: While they have blue in their name, great blue herons are really more gray than blue. They have a white head with a dark feathery swoosh over the eye on both sides. Males and females look alike.

Look on the left side of this tall evergreen tree. There's a nest with some young herons in it! An adult is also keeping watch over on the right.

SOUND: Most of the time, great blue herons stand silent, but they have several different squawking and clicking noises they make when threatened, meeting a mate, or calling to their chicks.

NEST & EGGS: Since you often see great blue herons when they're fishing, you might think their nest would be on the ground nearby. But great blue herons usually nest in the high branches of tall trees near water. They build huge nests (up to 4 feet across) out of sticks in colonies with lots of other herons and sometimes even with other wading birds like egrets. The female great blue heron may lay between two and six large pale blue eggs. Babies hatch out covered in gray down, looking even more like dinosaurs than their parents.

FOOD: The heron can curl its neck up like a letter *S* or extend it out straight to snap up a passing fish. While you can often spot them fishing, herons might also be hunting for other small critters they can snatch or stab with their long beak. They eat amphibians, small mammals, insects, and even small birds.

REGION & HABITAT: Great blue herons are found throughout most of North America. In the Pacific Northwest they live around bodies of both salt water and fresh water, everywhere from the Pacific coastline to backyard streams and inland ponds.

SEASON: Year-round.

A shorter and less outgoing cousin of the great blue heron is the green heron. If you look carefully among the plants at the edge of a pond, you might see one of these amazing birds. Smaller, shyer, and

Green heron

less common than their great blue cousins, these chestnut-and-teal-colored shorebirds are a great find for Pacific Northwest birders.

Grosbeak

In French the word *gros* means "big." So the grosbeak's name means "big beak." What a perfect name for this large-billed bird!

The two species of grosbeak you are most likely to see in the Pacific Northwest are the black-headed grosbeak and the evening grosbeak.

Black-headed Grosbeak

Male

SIZE: Grosbeaks are about 7½ inches long with a wingspan of about a foot. They are technically a type of finch, but birders tend to think of them as their own category. This is because a grosbeak is about the same size as a robin, which is much larger than other finches. (Read more about finches on page 107.)

Female

COLOR & PATTERN: This is another case where ornithologists named the species after the appearance of the male. The male black-headed grosbeak has a black head, eyes, back, and wings, with white bars on the wings and a gray bill. His underparts and neck are bright orange and yellow. (These birds are really beautiful when they fly.) The female is brown up above and softer orange underneath, with the same gray bill and dark eyes as the male.

SOUND: The black-headed grosbeak has a long, involved song that sounds a little like a robin but with more flair. Both the males and the females sing.

Fledgling

NEST & EGGS: Grosbeak nests can be tough to spot. The birds pick locations in trees near streams, well camouflaged by leaves and branches. The nests are 5 to 7 inches wide and kind of messy. The female grosbeak builds her nest out of small twigs, hair, thin roots, and even string—but no mud or other sealant of any kind. She lays two to five eggs in a clutch and has one brood per year. The eggs are pale bluish green with brown spots. Chicks hatch out naked and helpless. They need to spend about two weeks in the nest before they're ready to venture out.

FOOD: Grosbeaks enjoy both seeds and insects. Those giant beaks are perfect for cracking open sunflower seeds as well as the shells on crunchy beetles. They also enjoy small fruit, so you might see them in an orchard munching on figs or cherries too. You can encourage black-headed grosbeaks to come to your yard in the summertime by putting out feeders with black oil sunflower

seeds. (You could also put out beetles, but sunflower seeds are probably easier.)

REGION & HABITAT: Black-headed grosbeaks live all over the western part of the United States, southern Canada, and Mexico. They like areas with a mix of large trees and open spaces, particularly near the banks of a stream.

SEASON: You can see black-headed grosbeaks during their summer breeding season here in the Pacific Northwest. During the winter they migrate to warmer areas down in central Mexico.

Evening Grosbeak

Male

SIZE: Evening grosbeaks are a little smaller than black-headed grosbeaks, between 6½ and 7 inches long.

COLOR & PATTERN: These birds look a little like a tropical parrot that's been blown northward from its usual home in the rain forest. Males are yellow and black with a pale bill. They have a bright yellow stripe above their eyes and a white patch on each wing. The females are mostly gray, and their wings are black and white. Their bills are a soft seafoam-green color.

Female

SOUND: Evening grosbeaks got their name because early birders mistakenly thought they only came out to sing in the evening. The truth is, they don't really sing at all, but they do loudly call and chirp to each other throughout the day.

NEST & EGGS: These grosbeaks nest high up in trees. The female builds a flimsy nest that is about 5 inches across out of small twigs, thin roots, lichen, and pine needles. She lays between two and five light blue spotted eggs and can have more than one brood per season. Chicks hatch out helpless and partly naked.

FOOD: Evening grosbeaks eat insects, spiders, grubs, seeds, plant buds, and small fruit—more insects in the summer and seeds in the winter. They don't show up very often at feeders but may visit if you put out a tray of sunflower seeds. They may also visit your yard if you have maple trees because they love to lick the sweet sap from broken twigs.

Grosbeaks sometimes bite things that aren't food just to sharpen their giant beaks.

REGION & HABITAT: Although they're becoming less common, evening grosbeaks can be found across most of the United States and Canada. They like areas with a mix of large trees and open spaces, particularly near the banks of a stream.

SEASON: Evening grosbeaks migrate south sometimes when there aren't enough seeds in the conifer trees to keep them fed through the winter. But you have a chance of seeing them year-round in the Pacific Northwest.

Gull

A lot of people call these common white or gray birds seagulls, but the more accurate term is just plain gulls. (You don't just see them at the sea, do you?) Gulls aren't just one species of bird either. There are more than twenty different species of gulls in the Northwest. If you want to try to tell them apart, look for the details, including bill color, leg color, eye color, wing markings, and other slight differences. This can be challenging even for experienced birders, though, so be patient. Consider making little sketches on your life list to help you keep track of details when you're not sure.

SIZE: Gulls are medium to large birds—quite a bit bigger than a robin—but the size can vary depending on the species. Males tend to be larger than females. They have longish, sturdy bills and webbed feet.

Juvenile gull

COLOR & PATTERN: Gulls are mostly white or gray with light heads and gray wings and backs. They often have dark or striped patterns on the wings and/or tail. Juveniles are usually darker than adults and are mottled (kind of spotted) or striped. They lighten every year until they finally look like adults around age two.

SOUND: Gulls all have slightly different calls, but most make some version of a high whistling cry that birders say sounds like "keow" or "mew."

NEST & EGGS: Gulls scrape a nest area out on the ground and line it with grasses and feathers. They lay from one to three eggs per clutch, and those eggs can be about 3 inches long—about the size of a goose egg. Gulls nest in colonies (often with many different species) and return to the same location to breed year after year. Both the male and female gull take turns sitting on the nest to incubate the eggs (keep them warm). If it's really hot outside the adult might fly down to the water to get wet and cool down the eggs. Babies hatch out of their eggs with their eyes open and thick down all over their bodies. Baby gulls are ready to explore nearby after just a couple of days.

FOOD: Like many other birds, gulls will eat anything they can find, including fish, small crabs, and shrimp. Yum! Your picnic lunch? Double yum! Roadkill? Sure! Garbage at the local dump? Why not? In some places the gulls are so bold that they'll swoop down and take your food as you're lifting it to your own mouth.

Who knew? Some young gulls practice catching fish midair by grabbing, dropping, and catching sticks while flying.

REGION & HABITAT: Gulls can be found along coastlines and inland all over the world. You'll see them on the beach for sure. But you also might see them on the field at a local elementary school or in the parking lot at the mall.

SEASON: You can spot gulls year-round in the Northwest, particularly along the Pacific coast.

Who knew? In 1848, California gulls saved crops in Utah from a cricket infestation. A swarm of crickets were eating crops and threatening to destroy that year's harvest. The gulls flew in and ate all the crickets, making the farmers super grateful. In honor of that, the state of Utah—a totally land-locked state with no oceans or beaches—named the California gull the state bird.

Hawk

Look up sometime and watch a hawk gliding in slow circles as it rides warm air currents high in the sky—equal parts fierce hunter and laid-back observer. Like eagles, hawks are raptors that are active during the daytime—which is great because that means you have a good chance of seeing them.

The Pacific Northwest has many different kinds of hawks. Two species that live all across the region are Cooper's hawks and red-tailed hawks.

Cooper's Hawk

SIZE: These medium-sized hawks are about the same size as a crow, around 14 to 15 inches long with a wingspan between 24 and 36 inches. Like most hawks, the female is usually larger than the male.

COLOR & PATTERN: Adult Cooper's hawks are gray on top and white with reddish striping underneath. Their long tails are striped black and gray, and they have striking bright red eyes. Juvenile Cooper's hawks are brown on top with brown-streaked underparts. They have

Juvenile Cooper's hawk

yellow eyes, but as they mature, their eyes turn red like their parents'.

SOUND: Cooper's hawks tend to be mostly silent. Both the male and the female will make a loud "cack-cack-cack-cack-cack" call if they feel threatened or they're looking for a mate.

NEST & EGGS: The male Cooper's hawk builds the nest out of sticks about two-thirds of the way up a large tree. The female hardly helps at all. The nests are about 2½ feet across and are lined with flakes of tree bark. The female lays two to six eggs per clutch and has one clutch per season. Babies hatch out of their eggs covered in white down and weighing only as much as a slice of bread.

FOOD: Cooper's hawks eat mainly medium-sized birds about the size of a robin—such as doves, jays, and well . . . robins, but they will hunt small mammals as well.

Who knew? Cooper's hawks like to visit bird feeders. They aren't there to munch on the birdseed, though. They're hoping to catch a bird coming to feed. Keep an eye on the trees and bushes around your feeders to see if there are any predators joining in the bird-watch. If you're watching birds and suddenly they all just "explode" away into the bushes (called flushing in the bird world), that's a good sign that a Cooper's hawk may be nearby.

REGION & HABITAT: Cooper's hawks live all over the United States and parts of southern Canada. Unlike many raptors who only hunt in open fields, these amazing fliers can hunt through forests and woodlands.

They also stalk backyard bird feeders, so you can often spot them in neighborhoods and parks.

SEASON: Cooper's hawks are year-round residents from central Washington downward in the Pacific Northwest. North of that, you'll see these hawks during the summertime.

Red-tailed Hawk

SIZE: These hawks range from around 18 to 22 inches long. But the impressive part comes when they spread out their wings. Red-tailed hawks can have a wingspan up to about 52 inches. That's over 4 feet wide!

COLOR & PATTERN: There are several different-looking subspecies of this bird, but you're most likely to spot one that is brown on top (including the head) with white and brown streaks on its belly and short reddish tail feathers (although these may be hard to see if it's perched). Juveniles have more brown streaking on their underparts.

SOUND: The male red-tailed hawk makes a hoarse screaming call while it soars. Juveniles make a sort of wailing cry that sounds a bit like a gull.

Who knew? When you hear a bald eagle cry in a movie or on TV, it's probably a red-tailed hawk cry instead of an actual eagle. Why? These amazing hunters just sound fierce, and directors seem to prefer that chilling scream to the squeakier screech of an actual bald eagle.

NEST & EGGS: These hawks build their nests up in the treetops, where they can see all around to spot both food and threats. The nests themselves are tall—usually about 3 feet wide and sometimes over 6 feet tall—and are made of sticks. The female lays one to five eggs per clutch. Chicks hatch out helpless and tiny, weighing only as much as a couple of slices of bread.

FOOD: Red-tailed hawks eat mostly small mammals (such as mice, rabbits, and squirrels), but they'll also eat birds, snakes, and sometimes carrion.

REGION & HABITAT: Red-tailed hawks can be found all over North America in pretty much every type of open habitat. They need a little room to soar, so you probably won't see them deep in an old-growth forest. But look along highways, in parks, and near open fields—particularly up on tall utility poles—and eventually you should spot one of these impressive hawks.

Red-tailed hawk in flight

SEASON: These hawks live year-round in most of the Pacific Northwest and are around during the summer in Canada.

Hummingbird

Hummingbirds—often called hummers by birders—are fascinating and unusual birds, and we're lucky to have a few different kinds in the Pacific Northwest. The two most common species of hummingbirds in this region are the Anna's and the rufous.

Anna's Hummingbird

Male

Female

SIZE: Tiny at just under 4 inches long, the Anna's is actually the larger of our two Pacific Northwest humming-bird species. They only weigh about as much as a teaspoon of sugar!

COLOR & PATTERN: Anna's hummingbirds' bodies and wings are metallic green and gray. The male has a flashy reddish-pink head, and the female has that same flashy reddish pink (and a little green in certain lighting) in a much smaller spot at her throat.

Who knew? Hummingbirds are only found in the Americas, not in the rest of the world. But the Anna's hummingbird was actually named after the beautiful French princess Anna de Belle Masséna. Her husband was an amateur ornithologist with an impressive bird collection. René Lesson, a famous naturalist (nature explorer) went to France to see the Masséna collection and decided to name the beautiful American hummingbird after the lovely French lady.

SOUND: Anna's hummingbirds do quietly chirp and sing, but you're much more likely to hear the buzzing, humming noise made by their wings and tails. Christopher Columbus wrote in his journals that he thought these buzzing birds must be some kind of bird-insect crossover. (They're not.)

Who knew? Hummingbird hearts beat about 1,200 times per minute. (Yours beats 60 to 200 times per minute depending on what you're doing.) Whew!

NEST & EGGS: Anna's hummingbird nests are tiny and well camouflaged. The female sits on a branch and builds the nest around her out of spider silk and soft plant fibers. She then camouflages the outside of the nest by decorating it with bits of local plants and lichen. Always be careful around places these nests might be since they're tiny and really hard to spot. Don't disturb shrubs and brambles in the spring, when these little beauties will be building their hidden homes. Anna's hummingbirds lay two tiny white eggs per clutch and can have up to three broods in a single season. Give them time to use that nest as often as they need it.

FOOD: Hummingbirds eat flower nectar, spiders, midges, and other tiny insects. We think of them as nectar eaters, but insects and spiders are just as important to a hummingbird's diet as flowers.

Check out that tongue! That long bill that looks like a straw doesn't actually work like one. Instead of sucking like you would on a straw, a hummingbird sticks its long tongue into the flower or feeder and laps up the nectar. The end of the hummingbird's tongue is forked. It spreads out inside a flower or feeder to pump nectar into the hummer's mouth.

REGION & HABITAT: Up until about the 1930s, Anna's hummingbirds were only found down in southern California and Mexico. Over the course of the last ninety years or so, their range has expanded north all the way to Canada. Scientists think this may be because of backyard feeders and gardeners planting non-native plants such as eucalyptus trees. These hummingbirds like scrublands and open woods, but they can just as often be seen around suburban backyards. In 2017 the Anna's hummingbird was chosen as the official bird of Vancouver, British Columbia—a long way from its original southern range.

SEASON: Anna's hummingbirds are a year-round resident in most of the Pacific Northwest—especially along the coast. They are a fantastic reason to get out and go birding during the wintertime.

Rufous Hummingbird

Male

Female

SIZE: The tiny rufous hummingbird is only around 2½ to 3½ inches long, but it makes up for its small size with a big attitude. They'll guard feeders and other choice territory from other hummingbirds and anyone else who might seem like a threat.

COLOR & PATTERN: Rufous hummingbirds have beautiful orange and green feathers. The word *rufous* actually means "reddish brown," and you can see it in a lot of bird descriptions to indicate an orange color. The male is more orange all over with hints of green, while the female is mostly green with hints of orange on her belly, back, and tail. The adult male has flashy red iridescent feathers all over his throat.

SOUND: Rufous hummingbirds don't sing, but these fierce little birds will make warning "chip" sounds as they dive at trespassers in their territory. Their wings produce one of the loudest hums of all hummingbird species. They can even control how high or low the hum sounds by changing how fast they flap their wings. Rufous hummingbird wings can flap as fast as fifty to sixty times every second!

Rufous hummingbird nestlings

NEST & EGGS: Hummingbird nests are tiny and well camouflaged. Only a little bigger than a walnut shell, they're made out of fluffy plant fibers, lichen, moss, and spider silk. The nests are soft and squishy, and they actually stretch as the babies get bigger. Rufous hummingbirds usually lay between two and three eggs that look like little white jelly beans. The babies hatch out naked except for a few just-starting pin feathers, and they're ready to leave the nest (fledge) in less than three weeks. Rufous hummingbirds only have one brood per season.

REMEMBER THE BIRDER'S PLEDGE!

The photos in this book were all taken with special long lenses and setups that let the photographer take close-up photos without bothering the birds. If you see baby birds in a nest, especially hatchlings and nestlings, please stand far enough away that the bird parents don't feel threatened by you. Also, remember that smart birds like corvids might be watching when you look at a nest, which then points them toward a target they might attack.

FOOD: Even though they drink a lot of nectar with their beaks looking like they're almost closed, hummingbirds can open their beaks just like other birds. Sometimes you can even see them open wide to catch raindrops or tiny flying insects. They also find sapsucker holes (see page 201) to sip the sap and eat the insects they find there.

REGION & HABITAT: Rufous humming-birds migrate from north to south over a broad swath of western North America. Every year the tiny rufous hummingbird flies all the way from Alaska to Mexico and back again. These little hummingbirds can be seen in open areas such as meadows, swamps, parks, and yards. They need trees or shrubs for their nests, so look for them around forest edges too.

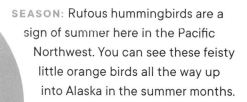

SEASON: Rufous hummingbirds are a sign of summer here in the Pacific Northwest. You can see these feisty little orange birds all the way up into Alaska in the summer months.

Who knew? Hummingbirds are the only birds that can fly backward! You can watch them hover in front of you, buzzing back and forth like a tiny helicopter.

Hummingbird Nectar: Simple Sipping Syrup

Hummingbirds burn a lot of calories as they flit about your yard. They need to eat about half their weight in sugar and bugs every day. That means they spend a lot of time drinking nectar from flowers. You can help—especially in the winter, when flowers are scarce—by hanging up a feeder filled with sugar water (nectar). Be sure to keep the feeder clean, and check it regularly to see if it needs a refill or a wash.

4 cups water

1 cup sugar

That's it! Hummingbirds don't need extras like coloring or weird flavors. And they don't need a special mix bought at the store. Simple really is best.

1   Boil the water on the stove or in the microwave. Add the sugar, stirring frequently until it dissolves. Let cool, then pour into a hummingbird feeder.

2   Keep an eye on your feeders, especially during warm weather. If the sugar-water solution starts to look cloudy or you see signs of mold, dump it out and wash the feeder. No matter what, give your hummingbird feeders a rinse in hot water every few days.

Who knew?
Hummingbirds are brave! They fiercely protect their feeders from other birds and will sometimes even approach when you're holding a feeder in your hand.

Killdeer

This is a striking shorebird you can see not just along the coast, but throughout the Pacific Northwest, both near water and on grassland (including lawns and golf courses).

SIZE: Killdeer are usually around 8 to 11 inches long, with long spindly legs and wings.

COLOR & PATTERN: Killdeer are mostly brown with white foreheads, eyebrow markings, and underparts. They have two bold black stripes across their chest and another stripe that goes across the crown of their head and through each eye. The eyes are dark with a deep-red ring around each one. Because of those eyes, killdeer always look surprised to see you.

SOUND: This bird gets its name from the loud call it makes that sounds a bit like "kill-deer!" No actual deer were harmed in the naming of the killdeer.

Can you see the difference between the baby in this picture and the adult above? The baby has only one stripe across its chest instead of two.

NEST & EGGS: Killdeer don't build nests but lay their eggs in little scrapes on the bare ground out in the open—often in gravel or on other hard surfaces. They gather stones, trash, and shells around their eggs once they're laid. Mama killdeer lay four to six eggs per clutch and can have up to three broods per year. The eggs are cream colored with a lot of dark brown or blackish spots. Babies hatch out covered with down, ready to leave the nest as soon as their feathers are dry. That's probably a good thing too, since the "nest" is made of hard rocks and shells.

Who knew? One of the most interesting behaviors of this bird is how it protects its young from predators. The adult will pretend to have a broken wing, dragging it behind as it leads the threat away from the nest. Since the nest is usually pretty unprotected, it's a good thing that these birds have developed such an impressive act to keep their babies safe!

FOOD: Killdeer eat mostly worms, snails, and insects. They'll also eat seeds from farmland.

REGION & HABITAT: Killdeer are technically shorebirds, but you can find them both near water and on dry land. They live all over the United states and Canada, even in places that don't have any kind of shore. You can find them in grassy areas, fields, or mudflats. Look for them especially if you see a muddy area near a pond or a stream.

SEASON: While some killdeer do migrate, here in the Pacific Northwest we have a lot of year-round residents. Look for them in the winter at a local wetlands.

Lazuli Bunting

Male

The bright, gemlike male lazuli bunting looks like an escaped pet next to most of our more softly colored local birds. But surprise, they're native here! Lazuli (rhymes with "as-you-lie") buntings were named after a pretty blue gemstone called lapis lazuli.

SIZE: Lazuli buntings are small birds, about the same size as a finch, around 5 to 6 inches long.

Female

COLOR & PATTERN: This little finchlike bird is another example where the male is much more brightly colored than the female. The male lazuli bunting is bright turquoise blue with black-and-white striping on his wings, and he has an orange-and-white breast. The female is a quiet grayish brown with slightly darker brown wings. She's a classic LBB (little brown bird), while her mate is a flashy blue show bird.

SOUND: Like many other songbirds, only the male lazuli bunting truly sings. Both sexes call to each other with a quick "pick pick" sound. Males learn to sing from other males, and each bird develops his own special tune. In the same way that people from different areas of the United States and Canada have very different accents, buntings have slightly different dialects from neighborhood to neighborhood.

NEST & EGGS: The female lazuli bunting weaves a nest in low-lying shrubs out of grass, leaves, bark, and spider silk. She lays three to four pale blue eggs per brood and sometimes has more than one brood per season. Chicks hatch mostly naked except for a little gray down along their spine.

FOOD: Lazuli buntings eat insects and spiders that they pick off the ground or from low-lying leaves and branches. They also eat seeds and berries. You can bring these colorful summer visitors to your yard by putting out a bird feeder with a mix of standard birdseed that includes white millet (the small, round, light-colored seeds in birdseed blends).

REGION & HABITAT: Lazuli buntings tend to appear inland rather than along the coast of our region. If you're lucky they will join finches and juncos at your backyard feeder. Cross your fingers and have your binoculars ready!

SEASON: You can see these little gems in the summertime over much of the Pacific Northwest.

Male (left) and juvenile or female (right) lazuli bunting.

Mourning Dove

Mourning doves are one of the most common and widespread birds in North America. They have small heads and sleek, pale bodies and look a little like their city cousin, the pigeon.

The word *mourning* means "to feel sad when someone dies," and it's pronounced like *morning*, the first part of the day. Early birdwatchers heard the cry of the mourning dove and thought it sounded like the sad sound of someone missing a person who'd died.

SIZE: Mourning doves are about the size of a robin, usually between around 9 and 13 inches long.

COLOR & PATTERN: With pale grayish-beige bodies and black spots on their wings, mourning doves blend in well with their surroundings. Since they live in every type of ecosystem in North America, being softly colored and spotted—like a shadow or pebbles—helps them hide in all types of environments, especially on the ground where they feed.

SOUND: Often when you hear a "coo-hoo-hoo-hoo," you may think you're hearing an owl. More likely, especially if it's daytime, you're actually hearing a mourning dove.

NEST & EGGS: Mourning doves nest both in trees and on the ground. Sometimes, they even nest in the gutters on a house or on other manmade structures. The female builds the nest out of thin twigs, pine needles, and grass. Their nests aren't very strong or very snug, so the young (who are born helpless) rely on the parents to keep them warm after they hatch and until their feathers grow in. Many birds (including doves) may reuse their nests the following year, so it's always a good idea to look but leave nests where they are when you find them in the off-season. Mourning doves lay two little white eggs in each clutch, and they can have several broods in a single season.

FOOD: Doves are seed eaters. They peck around on the ground picking up seeds that they store in their crop. Later, they'll fly off to somewhere safer (like up in a tree) to digest their food slowly without the threat of being attacked. Both the male and the female feed their chicks crop milk, which is also called pigeon milk. *Guess what other type of bird feeds their young crop milk?* (See rock pigeons on page 163.) Find out more about crop milk on page 7.

REGION & HABITAT: Mourning doves are common throughout the United States and up into southern Canada. They like to feed in grasslands that have woods and shrubs around to provide shelter and safety. You can even find them in the desert as long as there's water somewhere within several miles. Mourning doves may visit any place they can get to an open edge. That means they aren't deep-forest birds, but you have a good chance of seeing them most other places you go.

Who knew? One reason you may find mourning doves in the desert is that they can drink water that's a little bit salty without getting sick. They can't drink water as salty as the ocean, but they are better adapted to drinking brackish (salty) water than a lot of other birds.

SEASON: Mourning doves can be seen year-round in most of the Northwest, and during the summer in western British Columbia.

A second type of dove you might see in the Pacific Northwest is the Eurasian collared dove. This dove is larger than a mourning dove, and it sports a black collar across the back of its neck. This dove is what we call a non-native species. That means it started out somewhere else (in this case, Europe and Asia)

Eurasian collared dove

and was brought to our area, where it thrived in the wild. Bringing non-native species to a new area can have a huge impact on the native plants and animals, even though this particular bird has not hurt native dove numbers. As you read through the other birds in this book, keep an eye out for other non-native species and how they're affecting the Pacific Northwest.

Osprey

Osprey—like eagles, hawks, and falcons—are raptors. In fact, the name osprey comes from the Latin term *avis prede*, which means "bird of prey."

SIZE: These impressive birds are smaller than bald eagles, but still larger than most birds in the Pacific Northwest. Ospreys' bodies are around 22 inches long, and their wingspan can be between 5 and 6 feet wide.

COLOR & PATTERN: Ospreys are dark brown on top and mostly white underneath. Their heads are white with a dark brown eye bar and a black beak. When you see one flying, the "wrists" (the joints in the middle of the wing) are dark brown and the wing feathers are noticeably striped with brown, while the body, throat, and legs are white.

Who knew? You can tell osprey from other raptors by the way they hold their wings when they fly. The wings bend slightly at the "wrist" while the bird is soaring, kind of looking like a scarecrow with its elbows slightly bent.

SOUND: The osprey's call is a high, whistling chirp that sounds like "kee kee kee." If it's alarmed, an osprey will chirp loudly many times in a row.

Osprey babies grow quickly, so don't be surprised to see a squawking youngster begging for food from a parent who doesn't look a whole lot bigger than the baby. Remember to look for fluffier feathers and streaking to identify a juvenile. Also, be sure to check out the eyes. Juveniles' eyes are orange-red, but they change to pure yellow as adults. Doesn't the parent in this photo look ready for a break from all the squawking?

NEST & EGGS: Osprey's huge nests are made of sticks lined with grass, moss, and bark. In addition to trees and snags, you can often spot their impressive nests on cell phone towers and billboards. These raptors like to perch up high, with a clear view of the area around them. Osprey generally mate for life and return to the same nest year after year. The female lays one to four cream-colored and burgundy-spotted eggs per clutch, and the babies hatch out covered in down. Most baby raptors look like tiny fuzzy dinosaurs.

FOOD: Osprey eat pretty much only fish. They hunt by plunging feetfirst into water to catch fish swimming near the surface.

The owners of this billboard worried about the annual osprey nests making it hard for workers to do their jobs. So they built the osprey their very own platform even higher than the billboards! The osprey love their new higher perch, and the workers can safely access the walkways. It's a win for everyone!

Who knew? Osprey are different from other raptors because they have one toe on each foot that can rotate from the front to face backward. That allows them to have two toes in front and two behind so they can grab and hold giant, slippery fish from a river.

REGION & HABITAT: Osprey live on every continent in the world except Antarctica. Since they're fish eaters, they need to live somewhere near water. Any type of water with fish will do—rivers, ponds, oceans, and lakes are all great spots to look for osprey.

SEASON: Osprey migrate south in the winter, so the best time to see them in the Pacific Northwest is in the spring and summer. That's great for birders because it means they're in our area for breeding season.

Owl

Owls are birds of prey with a few cool features that set them apart from other raptors. For example, many owls have their ears at different heights on their head (even if you can't see them)—the left and right sides don't match. Amazingly, that slight difference in ear height lets them hear their prey's location precisely. Added to their sharp eyesight, it makes owls amazing predators. Often nocturnal (active at night), you are much more likely to hear an owl calling than you are to see one.

Barred owl

The Pacific Northwest has many different kinds of owls. Two types that you may spot are the barred owl and the western screech-owl. (Also check out the great horned owls on page 10.)

Who knew? Have you ever seen a video of an owl turning its head almost all the way around? That's an adaptation that makes up for the fact that owls' eyes aren't round—they're tube-shaped! Their eyes actually don't move like ours at all. Owls have to turn their head if they want to look side to side. And wow, can they ever turn their heads. Owls can rotate their heads up to 270 degrees—that's three-fourths of the way around!

Barred Owl

SIZE: Barred owls are fairly large, ranging from around 17 to 19½ inches long with a wingspan of up to 43 inches across.

COLOR & PATTERN: Barred owls are streaked brown and white overall. Their breasts are striped brown and white (from side to side) while their bellies are striped up and down. It kind of looks like a striped shirt and pants. This owl also has barring (horizontal stripes) on its back and wings.

SOUND: The barred owl makes a loud hooting call that sounds a bit like "who cooks for you."

NEST & EGGS: Barred owls nest in tree cavities, laying their eggs right on the surface of whatever wood has been carved or rotted away. They can lay one to five white eggs per clutch, and the chicks hatch out covered in fine white down.

FOOD: Like most other owls, barred owls hunt small animals such as mice, birds, moles, chipmunks, frogs, and snakes. They'll eat insects, and sometimes they'll even hunt fish. Occasionally they'll even prey on other owls.

While different owls eat different-ent sizes of prey, they all share one cool eating behavior in common: they swallow their food whole or in large chunks and then regurgitate the stuff they can't digest as a pellet. Check out the information on owl pellets on page 156.

REGION & HABITAT: Barred owls used to be found only on the East Coast. Over the last hundred years, though, they've moved north and west. Now they compete with threatened spotted owls in Pacific Northwest forests. Like spotted owls, they prefer old-growth forests, a habitat that is shrinking due to logging and other human activities.

Northwest birders often aren't sure if they should be excited or upset when they see this owl. Invasive species frustrate birders when they mess with populations of native birds. But this owl wasn't brought in by humans. It arrived here on its own, and it looks like it's here to stay. *What do you think?*

SEASON: Year-round.

Juvenile barred owl

Western Screech-owl

SIZE: The western screech-owl is a small squarish owl about the size of a robin, but much fluffier and with almost no neck.

COLOR & PATTERN: Here in the Pacific Northwest, western screech-owls are reddish brown with darker and lighter vertical striping that makes them almost perfectly match the tree bark where they spend their days. They have a dark border around their face, a dark beak, and yellow eyes.

SOUND: The screech-owl has a distinctive hooting call that starts out slowly and speeds up as it goes along—"hoot . . . hoot . . . hoot . . . hoot-hoot-hoot-hoot."

NEST & EGGS: Western screech-owls are cavity nesters. They often depend on woodpeckers to drill them a home, but then the owls may use the same nesting cavity for several years in a row. Like the barred owl, this owl doesn't build a nest. The female just lays her eggs straight onto the floor of the cavity. She can lay from two to seven white eggs per clutch, and the chicks—called owlets—will hatch out covered in white down. The male provides all of the food for the mama and the nestlings during the nesting period.

FOOD: Screech-owls are nocturnal hunters. They glide silently through the night looking for small mammals and other critters to eat. Their favorites are small animals such as mice, rats, and even bats.

REGION & HABITAT: Yes, there is also a bird called an eastern screech-owl, and it's a lot like this one. But the two separate species live on opposite coasts and don't overlap in their ranges. If you see a screech-owl in the Pacific Northwest, it's a western screech-owl.

Western screech-owls like deciduous forests best. That makes sense since they look so much like tree bark! But unlike most owls, they are also fairly tolerant of people. That means you might see or hear one at a park or playground near you.

SEASON: Year-round.

Who knew? Another thing all owl species have in common is that they are almost silent fliers. Owl wings have serrated feathers on the front edge that help these hunters cut silently through the wind. The rest of the downy feathers on an owl's wings also help to muffle sound. One could fly right by you and you might not hear it. This gives owls a big advantage when they are swooping down on their prey.

One group of Northwest kids found a western screech-owl and her baby living in the top of the covered area on their school's playground. The sound of kids running and playing at recess doesn't seem to bother the owls at all. Sometimes the owls sit and watch the students play basketball!

Owl Pellet Dissection

Owls gulp down their prey whole or close to it. They don't even bother to pluck out feathers and fur first! Their bodies can't digest everything they swallow, though. Things like bones, fur, beaks, feathers, and teeth collect in the gizzard and are pressed together into a hard pellet about the size of an adult human thumb. Usually about once a day, the owl regurgitates this pellet onto the ground. If you look down under an owl's favorite roosting spot, you can often find owl pellets in various stages of decay. If you collect and dissect these before they decompose, you can learn a lot about the owl that coughed them up and what it's been eating.

You can buy sterile owl pellets online.

YOU'LL NEED:

An owl pellet (see Note, opposite)
Tweezers
Wooden probe (a bamboo kitchen skewer works great)
A paper plate or clean piece of paper

The bone identification chart on page 159
Handheld magnifying glass (optional but fun; little plastic lenses are fine)

1. After sterilizing, unwrap your pellet and discard the foil.

2. Use tweezers, your fingers, and your wooden probe to gently pry apart the pellet until you start to see bones and other animal parts.

3. Use your tools to gently remove interesting parts and set them aside on your plate or a clean piece of paper. Go slowly. Remember, this is your own private dinosaur dig. You don't want to destroy the bones and other interesting bits you may find inside.

4. Once you've discovered all the treasures hidden in your pellet, use a bone chart or other guide to try to figure out what the owl has been eating.

5. If you want to keep and display the bones you found, you can glue them down on cardboard in the shape of the animal that was eaten.

IMPORTANT NOTE: If you find your own owl pellets out in the wild, be sure to wear gloves when picking them up. Before you dissect any pellets you collect, sterilize them by wrapping each one separately in a strip of foil and baking them in the oven at 325 degrees F for 40 minutes. That will kill any harmful germs. Let them cool before handling.

Your parents may be happy to learn that you can also buy sterilized owl pellets cheaply online from many different sources. Just search for "owl pellets" in your web browser. Either way, be sure to wash your hands well after this activity. (They're sterilized, but it's still technically owl barf.) If you're squeamish, you can wear disposable latex gloves, but it's fine to dissect sterilized owl pellets with your bare hands.

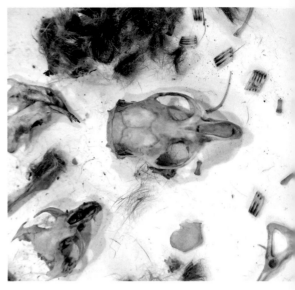

What kind of animal do you think this owl has been eating?

But why on earth would I want to collect owl barf? These pellets are actually a fascinating way to investigate what an owl has been eating. Since owl stomachs aren't as acidic as a lot of other birds', the bones and fur that come back out are often in perfect condition for identification. You need to sterilize the pellets first, but after that, it's a non-smelly, super-interesting, and not-at-all gross hands-on science investigation. Think of it as your own miniature dinosaur bone dig.

Bone Identification Chart

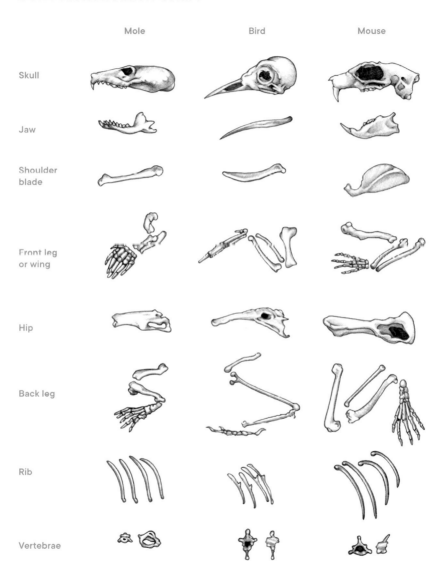

	Mole	Bird	Mouse
Skull			
Jaw			
Shoulder blade			
Front leg or wing			
Hip			
Back leg			
Rib			
Vertebrae			

Red-breasted Nuthatch

Red-breasted nuthatches are the downward-moving counterparts to upward-moving brown creepers (see page 71). While brown creepers move *up* tall trees looking for insects and spiders, nuthatches scurry *down* trees looking for similar snacks. Nuthatches also enjoy nuts and seeds. Even when they eat from feeders, these little birds are often upside down. You can also see them arch their backs to almost a 90-degree angle to look behind them. It's a very distinctive nuthatch pose and makes them easy to identify.

SIZE: These small birds average a little over 4 inches long.

COLOR & PATTERN: Red-breasted nuthatches actually have more of a soft rust-colored breast than a red one, and it's paler on females than on males. Their backs are blue-gray, and they have white eyebrows and a black bar across each eye.

SOUND: Red-breasted nuthatches have a sharp, quick, chattering call that sounds a little like "yank yank yank."

If the body style and behavior say "nuthatch" to you, but you don't see that rusty breast or the black eye bar, you might actually be seeing a white-breasted nuthatch, which is a close cousin.

White-breasted nuthatch

Juvenile red-breasted nuthatch

NEST & EGGS: Nuthatches are cavity nesters, so you probably won't see their actual nest. If you're lucky, though, you may see the female collecting fine grasses or even fur to line it. Both the male and the female dig out the nest hole. Then the female builds the nest inside. Nuthatches rarely use bird-houses—they're more do-it-yourself birds. The female lays between two and eight eggs per clutch. The eggs are cream colored to pinkish with brown speckles. Babies hatch out naked.

Who knew? Nesting red-breasted nuthatches set traps for intruders! Both the male and the female nuthatch smear sticky pitch on the outside of their nest hole to keep uninvited visitors from coming in. The nuthatches know it's there and can avoid it when they enter, but it can cause quite a mess for intruders.

FOOD: Red-breasted nuthatches eat both insects and seeds. They hunt for tiny insects in the crevices of tall conifer trees and love a juicy spider to feed to their young. They will also visit seed and suet feeders, so you could definitely see one in your yard if you put out feeders for them.

Who knew? Sometimes red-breasted nuthatches store food in the crevices of tree bark. You never know when a hungry squirrel or woodpecker might stumble upon a stash, though, so this is a little risky for the nuthatch.

REGION & HABITAT: Red-breasted nuthatches can be found all over the United States and Canada. They like coniferous forests, but they can also be seen in wooded parks and yards in the Pacific Northwest.

SEASON: Year-round.

Rock Pigeon

Rock pigeons are some of the most common city birds across North America, but they aren't originally from here. They were brought by settlers in the early 1600s. At that time there was a native pigeon living in North America called the passenger pigeon. It was once the most abundant bird in North America, but sadly it's now extinct because it was overhunted by people. Rock pigeons now live in the places where native passenger pigeons used to thrive.

SIZE: Rock pigeons are bigger and chubbier than similar-looking mourning doves, usually around 12 to 14 inches long.

COLOR & PATTERN: Like hummingbirds, rock pigeons often have iridescent feathers around their necks. While many rock pigeons have a blue-gray body with two dark stripes on each wing, the actual color combinations can

vary widely. Watch for pinkish-red legs and feet, and rich purples and greens around their necks. The white spot that looks like a split mini marshmallow on top of their beak is called the cere (pronounced "seer"), and it is where their nostrils are.

SOUND: Rock pigeons make an assortment of cooing sounds.

NEST & EGGS: These pigeons are named after the rocky ledges where they build their nests in the wild. In cities, rock pigeons nest on the next best thing to rock cliffs: ledges on tall buildings, towers, and bridges. The female builds the nest out of twigs and straw brought to her by the male. Rock pigeons don't clean their babies' poop out of their nests like most

other birds do. And they often use their nests year after year. Eventually, the nest becomes a big sturdy bowl made of twigs and poop. Females lay one to three eggs per clutch and can have up to *six* broods per season. No wonder there are so many pigeons in cities!

Who knew? Pigeons, like doves, make nutritious crop milk for their young. See more about crop milk on page 7. Up until 2003, rock pigeons were actually called rock doves. Those ornithologists like to keep us on our toes as we try to memorize bird names!

FOOD: Mostly seed eaters, rock pigeons—like many other city-dwelling birds—are also opportunists. If you decide to feed pigeons in your yard or a city park, only toss out as much birdseed as they can eat right away, or you may attract another type of opportunistic feeder: rats.

REGION & HABITAT: Rock pigeons can be found virtually all over the world, especially in large cities. These birds have adapted well to living with people. You can often see them in flocks pecking the ground for handouts or discarded food along sidewalks, parks, and open lots in cities. In more natural areas you can look for them along rocky cliffs, which is how they got their name after all.

> **Who knew?** Pigeons are great at finding their way home from distant locations. Humans discovered this and have used that fact to train pigeons to deliver messages. Pigeons have been living with (and delivering messages for) humans for thousands of years, all the way back to ancient Egypt. Rock pigeons were even used by the military in World Wars I and II to carry secret messages to and from the troops.

SEASON: Year-round.

Band-tailed pigeon

If you visit the forests of the Pacific Northwest in the summertime, you might see another impressive local pigeon—the band-tailed pigeon. These are less common than their city cousins, but they do sometimes visit backyard bird feeders for a snack. They're larger and less colorful than rock pigeons, and they have a distinctive white band across the back of their neck.

Sparrow

Do you see a little brown bird on the ground? Odds are it may be a sparrow of some kind. Sparrows are seed-eating songbirds that are often seen and heard at backyard feeders. There are more than twenty different species of sparrows living throughout the Pacific Northwest, many of them year-round. A couple of common sparrows found in the Pacific Northwest are profiled here, but there are too many to describe in a short section. Keep a notebook handy in case you see something similar but just a little different while you're birding.

Song Sparrow

SIZE: These small songbirds range from around 4½ inches to 7½ inches. That's a pretty big range, so you'll want to pay attention to features other than just size to make an identification.

COLOR & PATTERN: This common streaked brown sparrow is another classic LBB (little brown bird). It has brown and gray streaks above with a lighter streaked chest and underparts. Even its bill is kind of brownish gray. Many other species of sparrow are sort of brown and streaky, but if it's just brown and gray with no other marks, you're probably seeing a song sparrow. Males and females look alike.

SOUND: Song sparrows, as their name suggests, will sit on a low branch and serenade you with a long twittering song. If they're scared by a predator (or you), they'll make a loud "chip" call.

NEST & EGGS: Both the male and the female help choose the nest site in tall grasses, shrubs, or even in your garden. (These birds are pretty relaxed around people.) The female builds her cup-shaped nest out of grasses, weeds, bark, and even animal hair. She'll lay between one and six blue-green eggs with brown or purple spots, and she often lays more than one clutch per season. The babies will hatch out naked except for a little black fuzzy down.

FOOD: Song sparrows are mostly seed eaters, but they will also eat insects, especially in the summer when they are feeding babies. Like many birds, they tend to feed on what's most available wherever they are.

REGION & HABITAT: These little birds are found all over North America wherever there's any green space at all for them. Look for them in any park, garden, or nature trail.

SEASON: Year-round.

White-crowned Sparrow

SIZE: These little birds are just about 6 inches long.

COLOR & PATTERN: The bright white-and-black stripes on its head make the white-crowned sparrow an easy bird to identify. Its neck and underparts are a soft gray while its back and wings are striped in brown. Male and female white-crowned sparrows look alike, but the juveniles can be a bit tricky. Instead of being white and black, the stripes on a youngster's head are brown and gray.

SOUND: The song of the white-crowned sparrow is a series of clear, sweet notes followed by a jumble of whistles and trills.

NEST & EGGS: These sparrows usually nest in low shrubs, but they will also nest on the ground, well hidden by vegetation. The female builds her cup-shaped nest out of grasses, bark, moss, and dead leaves. Then she lines it with soft grass and/or animal hair. She will lay three to six pale green, brown-spotted eggs per clutch and can have more than one clutch per season. Babies are born

*White-crowned sparrow
nest and eggs*

Juvenile white-crowned sparrow

almost naked, helpless, and weighing about as much as a penny.

FOOD: White-crowned sparrows eat weeds and grass seeds as well as insects. They will also come to backyard feeders to help clean up fallen seeds other birds have spilled to the ground.

REGION & HABITAT: When they're in the Pacific Northwest, white-crowned sparrows especially like thickets where they can easily hide among the branches. You can also find them in fields, parks, and suburban yards. Up in the far northern parts of Canada and Alaska, where they commonly breed, they can be found on the tundra and alpine meadows.

SEASON: This sparrow is most common in the wintertime in the Pacific Northwest, except along the coast and a few patches inland where you can see it year-round.

If you spot a bird that looks a lot like a white-crowned sparrow but with bright yellow where the white head stripe should be, it's probably a golden-crowned sparrow. Try to notice as many details like this as possible when you're identifying a bird.

Golden-crowned sparrow

Spotted Towhee

Male

The spotted towhee is a large, shy sparrow that stands out because of its striking coloring and startling red eyes.

SIZE: About the same size as a robin—bigger than most other sparrows, which is why they are usually grouped separately— spotted towhees average around 7 to 8 inches long.

Female

COLOR & PATTERN: Male spotted towhees have black backs, beaks, and heads, rust-colored sides, and white bellies. Their wings are brightly spotted with white. Females look like the males, but everything is more subdued. Instead of black, their backs, wings, and heads are a dusty grayish brown. Both sexes have a hood that might remind you of a dark-eyed junco and red sides a little like a robin's breast.

Who knew? If one of your parents or grandparents is a birder, they may know this little guy as a rufous-sided towhee because of its reddish-brown sides. (Remember, that's what *rufous* means.) That species was split in two and renamed back in 1995.

SOUND: Spotted towhees make a sweet chirping "tweet, tweet" often followed by a trill.

NEST & EGGS: Like many other sparrows, spotted towhees nest on the ground. The female builds the nest out of stems, strips of bark, and dry leaves. Then she lines it with softer material like grass or hair. She will lay two to six small spotted eggs per clutch and can have up to three broods per season. Babies hatch out naked and helpless.

FOOD: Spotted towhees eat both plants and insects. In the summer when they're feeding their babies, spotted towhees will eat mostly high-protein insects. In the fall and winter they're more likely to eat seeds, berries, and acorns. Towhees are frequent visitors at backyard bird feeders, where they will stare back at you with their intense red-eyed glare.

REGION & HABITAT: Spotted towhees live all over the western United States and southwestern Canada. Like many other birds, they like living along forest edges, so look for them in open areas around trees. You can spot them down in the dead leaves on the ground doing a two-footed scoot forward and back to look for food.

SEASON: These are year-round birds in the Pacific Northwest. They are fun to look for in the winter, when they are easier to spot without the leaf cover they use to hide. It's also when you're most likely to see one all fluffed up like a little ball to keep warm. It's tough to look fierce when you're a puffball!

Starling

Starlings are smart and pretty, but they're also a really good example of how people can mess up the natural world without meaning to. Back in 1890 a group of people released a small flock of starlings in New York City's Central Park. Some say it was to bring every bird mentioned in Shakespeare to the New World. Other people say it was to "civilize" the wild land with pieces of home. Bringing living things from other lands to America wasn't uncommon back then, but this species succeeded here past everyone's expectations. The one hundred birds released in New York back in 1890 have reproduced and spread, and there are now more than 200 million starlings living all over North America!

SIZE: Starlings are medium-sized birds (like a robin). They measure about 8 inches long from head to tail.

COLOR & PATTERN: Both male and female starlings look mostly black until you see them in the light. Check out the iridescent purple, blue, and green in their feathers! In the wintertime, their feathers fade a little and are covered with white spots—like snow.

SOUND: Starlings make a wide range of sounds (chirps, whistles, and chatters), and they can even imitate other birds. Sometimes when you think you're hearing a certain bird's call, it's really a starling being an amazing copycat.

NEST & EGGS: Starlings almost always build their nests in a cavity. If you look closely at old woodpecker holes, birdhouses, or other protected dark spaces, you might see a parent bringing snacks to some hungry babies. The male starts building the nest in the cavity before mating, filling it up with grasses, trash, feathers, string, and other soft bits and pieces he finds. The female has the final say on what stays in the nest before laying three to six light bluish eggs per clutch. She can have more than one brood per season, but the hatchlings need a lot of care. They don't even open their eyes for a week after they hatch.

Starlings are also one of those birds where the babies look very little like the parents. Look at this little beige juvenile! Yup, that's a starling.

Unfortunately, when you introduce a new species into an ecosystem that isn't used to it, something has to give. In this case, starlings often take all of the best nesting cavities, leaving western bluebirds and other cavity-nesting native birds out of luck for good places to raise their young. You can tell by the band on this

Western bluebird

bluebird's ankle that an ornithologist somewhere is keeping track of him to see how his local population is doing.

FOOD: Starlings will eat almost anything, but their favorite food is bugs. Do you see that long, bug-eating beak? Insects and spiders and worms are tasty treats, but starlings also won't pass up fruit, grains, or even your family's trash.

REGION & HABITAT: European starlings started in Europe, but they can now be spotted on every continent except Antarctica. In just 130 years they have spread out to become common all across North America. Starlings love to live around people. They use our buildings and structures for nesting, and they hunt for grubs in freshly mowed lawns.

SEASON: Year-round.

Who knew? Starlings often gather together in large flocks of thousands of birds. When they fly, they swoop and move in a rippling blob shape called a murmuration. Do an internet search for "starling murmuration video" to watch one of these amazing bird swarms in action.

Steller's Jay

What's blue and a jay but not a blue jay? A Steller's jay, of course! Jays belong to the same big family as crows and ravens—they're all corvids. And like other corvids, Steller's jays are smart and loud and curious.

These gorgeous dark blue and black jays have a distinctive crest on their head that helps you identify them easily. They also have a bit of a reputation as backyard bird bullies. If you have a Steller's jay at your feeder (or more likely, several of them), you'll be able to hear it from a ways off.

Who knew? Steller's jays were named after Georg Steller, an eighteenth-century naturalist. You may also have seen Steller's sea lions, which were named after him too. Some people misspell this jay's name as *stellar*, a word that means "great." But while these jays are indeed pretty great, they're Steller, not stellar.

SIZE: Steller's jays are between 11 and 13 inches from tip to tail. They're a bit smaller than their crow cousins but still pretty impressive for backyard birds.

COLOR & PATTERN: Steller's jays have dark blue bodies with a black head and crest (the triangle-shaped mohawk of feathers on top of its head). They also have a couple of vertical slashes of blue on their forehead between their eyes. Fledglings and juveniles are paler gray on top, and if they're young enough you may be able to see the pink gape flange at the base of their beak. Their feathers darken as they get older.

Juvenile Steller's jay

SOUND: Steller's jays are extremely loud, make a wide variety of calls, and have even been known to imitate other animals (both birds and mammals). The Steller's jay's main call is often described as sounding like "shook, shook, shook, shook, shook!"

NEST & EGGS: Steller's jays build their nests in tall conifers such as pine and fir trees. Both the male and female gather sticks, leaves, other plant material, and mud to build their nest. Nests can be up to 17 inches across and 6 to 7 inches tall. The female lays from two to six eggs per clutch and has only one brood per season. Eggs are bluish green with brown spotting. Babies stay in the nest for two weeks after hatching.

FOOD: Like most other corvids, Steller's jays will eat whatever they can find, including insects, fruit, nuts, seeds, eggs, and the nestlings of other birds. They'll also steal food from other birds and people when they can.

If a Steller's jay comes to dine at your feeder, prepare for a dinner guest with no table manners at all. If he can't find the peanuts and larger seeds he craves, the Steller's jay will just dig through your regular birdseed until he finds something he likes, flinging the rest all over the place. If you have ground-feeding birds like sparrows or quails nearby, they will welcome the shower of seeds. But be prepared to refill your feeders often!

REGION & HABITAT: Steller's jays live in North America west of the Rocky Mountains. They can be found close to human cities and towns, but they prefer evergreen forests.

Depending on where you live, you may also see a variety of other members of this bird

family out in the forest. Along with the crows and ravens described on page 83, you may also spot California scrub jays (see below), Canada jays (formerly known as gray jays), pinyon jays, Clark's nutcrackers, and black-billed magpies.

SEASON: Steller's jays are year-round residents in the Northwest.

Another jay species you might spot in the Pacific Northwest is the California scrub jay. (Yeah, it says "California" in their name, but they live in parts of Oregon and Washington too.) California scrub jays are mostly a deep medium blue, lighter than their Steller's jay cousins, and they don't have the crest of feathers on their heads. Scrub jays also have light gray bellies and are slightly smaller than the Steller's jay, so it's easy to tell the two species apart from a distance.

California scrub jay

Swallow

Swallows are little birds without much of a neck. These amazing birds are like flying butterfly nets. They open their sharp, wide little beaks to catch flying bugs on the wing. They swoop gracefully up in the air, often diving down low to skim the surface of a lake or grassy field. Sometimes you can spot them resting on utility wires or the gutters of a house. There are seven different species of swallow in the Pacific Northwest. The details of the few included here will help you make a good guess at other similar species you see out in the wild. Once you can tell it's a swallow, pay attention to the field marks so you can see if it's one of these or something different for your life list.

Barn Swallow

SIZE: Barn swallows range from around 6 to 7½ inches long. Their tails are longer than their wings, and the male's tail is longer than the female's.

COLOR & PATTERN: Barn swallows have blue backs, orange bellies, and even darker reddish-orange throats. The female's underparts are much lighter than the male's, but her throat is still dark orange.

SOUND: Both males and females of this species sing. You may hear their long warbling song near a nest. You're more likely to hear a warning "cheep" or "churee," though, if the parents think you've gotten too close.

NEST & EGGS: Like their name suggests, barn swallows often nest in structures such as barns, sheds, and the eaves of buildings. The nests are made of mud and grass stems. Both the male and female gather mud and grass in their mouth, and then they spit out each glob to build up the sides of the

nest like bricklayers. Once it's built, the swallows line the mud cup with grass and feathers. The female lays three to seven pale speckled eggs per clutch and may have more than one clutch per season. Chicks hatch out helpless and almost naked.

Who knew? Some birds, including swallows, have a fascinating adaptation to keep their nests clean. When babies are really little, just nestlings, their poop comes out wrapped in soft little mucus bundles—

like little newborn bird diapers. The parents can fly the little bundles away so that predators can't tell there's a new baby in the nest. (Sometimes, to be honest, the parents might eat the bundles instead—but we don't need to think about that.)

FOOD: Barn swallows are insectivores, which means they eat insects—lots and lots of insects. Some swallows eat as many as sixty insects per hour. That's sixty fewer bugs in your yard every hour that a swallow is around! In the case of the barn swallow, most of these insects are flies.

REGION & HABITAT: Barn swallows breed all over the United States and Canada, and then they fly down to Central and South America for the winter. Barn swallows hunt for insects in open fields. They also need somewhere wet to get mud for building their nests. You may see them on farms, but you might also see them at a local park or on your soccer field at school.

SEASON: Like other swallows, these birds are spring and summer visitors to the Pacific Northwest, where they breed and raise their chicks.

Cliff Swallow

SIZE: These little swallows are only about 5 inches long.

COLOR & PATTERN: Cliff swallows have dark brownish wings and throats, blue backs, and orange rumps. Like many swallows, they are white underneath. Their faces are brick red, and their heads are blue with a white spot on their forehead. Males and females of this species look the same,

Juvenile cliff swallow

so if you see one that looks similar but with more muted coloring and a darker face, it's probably a juvenile.

SOUND: The most common sound made by cliff swallows is a soft purring "chur" call.

NEST & EGGS: Like barn swallows, cliff swallows build their nests out of mouthfuls of mud. You can often see colonies of these nests on both cliffs and the underside of bridges. The male and female make the nest together, and when it's finished it looks kind of gourd-shaped—like a pumpkin or squash—with an entrance hole near the top. The female lays one to six whitish eggs with brown speckles and can have more than one clutch per season.

Who knew? If a mama cliff swallow feels like she has too many eggs to incubate, she might grab one of them in her mouth and drop it into another cliff swallow's nest.

FOOD: Like other swallows, cliff swallows are insectivores. They hunt for flying insects in open fields, water bodies, and other flat, open areas that might attract swarms of insects.

REGION & HABITAT: Cliff swallows migrate all over North, Central, and South America. You can spot them from Alaska all the way down to the tip of Argentina. Like their name suggests, cliff swallows naturally live near the cliffs where they build their nests. Like many other cliff-dwelling birds (see peregrine falcon on page 104 for one example), they have adapted well to "cliffs" made by humans. Now you can find these little birds nesting on tall bridges and skyscrapers, so you don't even have to leave the city to find them.

SEASON: These swallows are summer visitors to the Pacific Northwest.

Violet-green Swallow

Male

Female

SIZE: These tiny birds are less than 5 inches long. Their wings are longer than their bodies, which you can clearly see while they're seated.

COLOR & PATTERN: Like many birds, violet-green swallows are darker on top and white below—including white cheeks. They have iridescent green shoulders and a purple rump. The white on their bellies wraps up around their hips, giving them what birders call saddlebags (a reference to the bags slung over horses). Males are usually more brightly colored than females, and they have a green cap on their head that matches their shoulders. Females have a pale brownish cap and duskier cheeks than the males. Their wings are long and pointed, and they have a slightly forked tail.

SOUND: Violet-green swallows are songbirds, but they only sing just before dawn. If you get up really early, you may hear them sing out a long series of chirps. During the day you're much more likely to hear their short calls: "chee chee!"

NEST & EGGS: These swallows are cavity nesters who lay their eggs in natural holes like those left by woodpeckers. They also use nesting boxes with small entrance holes. The male and female work together to build a shallow nest inside the cavity made of small twigs, grass, and feathers. The female lays four to six small white eggs per clutch and can have more than one clutch per season.

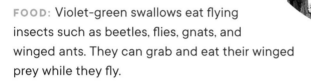

FOOD: Violet-green swallows eat flying insects such as beetles, flies, gnats, and winged ants. They can grab and eat their winged prey while they fly.

REGION & HABITAT: Violet-green swallows breed in the western half of the United States and Canada, and then they head south to Mexico and Central America for the winter. You may see these swallows flying over wetlands and lakes in lightly forested areas of the Northwest. They need dead trees with nesting cavities during breeding season, so seeing old snags—especially along the edge of a forest—increases the chance that

you'll see a violet-green swallow. These lovely birds may also stay in your yard if you put up a nesting box.

SEASON: Violet-green swallows are spring and summer visitors through-out the Pacific Northwest. They breed here and then migrate south for the winter. That means they're here for baby season!

Turkey Vulture

Turkey vultures are important in the natural environment because they are a feathered cleanup crew for dead things. When an animal dies, scavengers such as turkey vultures help to break down the carcass and return the nutrients to the soil. Turkey vultures got their names because they look a little like wild turkeys. But they don't actually sound anything like a turkey. *(Gobble, gobble.)*

SIZE: These are huge birds, up to almost 3 feet long, with a wingspan of up to around 5½ feet.

Who knew? Turkey vultures are pretty big for a bird, but even big animals have their attackers, especially when they're young. When vultures need to defend themselves, they vomit to scare off the threat. A big old stinky pile of stomach acid and decaying meat is usually enough to chase away even the most desperate predator.

COLOR & PATTERN: These dark brown birds have deep-red bald heads and pale-colored legs and beaks. Male and female adults look the same. Juveniles' heads are still naked, but they're gray instead of red; their legs and beaks are sort of grayish like their heads. Having no feathers on their head allows these birds to clean up easily after dining on a dead carcass.

Turkey vultures often stand with their wings spread wide open to soak up the sun. This helps warm their bodies and also destroys any bacteria that might cling to their feathers after

they feed. You can also tell this vulture is a juvenile because its head is not yet red.

SOUND: Surprise! Turkey vultures actually don't have vocal chords. If they're really upset, though, they might just hiss like a snake.

NEST & EGGS: Turkey vultures nest far away from human activity. It might be on a cliff, in a cave, or up in the branches of a tree—especially if there is an old hawk's nest there that they can use. Vultures don't actually build a nest on their own. They're more likely to scrape out a comfy spot in whatever place they've decided is safe. You're much more likely to see a turkey vulture soaring overhead than sitting on a nest. The female lays up to three large creamy-white eggs with purple or brown spots. The chicks hatch out defenseless, blind, and covered with soft down.

FOOD: Turkey vultures eat dead animals. They find carcasses with their amazing sense of smell. Even vultures don't want to eat old dead things that have started to rot, though, so they look for food that is newly dead.

REGION & HABITAT: Turkey vultures can be seen at least part of the year in most of the United States, southern parts of Canada, and down through Central America. You can spot vultures soaring over fields, highways, and other open spaces where there might be dead animals down below. The easiest ways to tell them apart from soaring raptors and ravens are to look for the spread "fingers" at the tips of their wings and to notice their back-and-forth wobble as they glide.

Who knew? Scavengers such as the turkey vulture have to deal with an added threat from hunting. It's illegal for people to shoot them directly, but they often get poisoned by eating lead shot from hunters' guns. Millions of birds are poisoned this way each year. Many groups—including the National Audubon Society, the American Bird Conservancy, and the Humane Society—are looking at ways to phase out the use of lead bullets because of the harm they do to animals and the environment.

SEASON: Turkey vultures are spring and summer visitors to the Pacific Northwest. The rest of the year they migrate south to parts of California as well as Central and South America.

Woodpecker

Woodpeckers are some of the most exciting birds to see (and hear) in the Pacific Northwest. We have both the smallest and the largest wood-peckers in North America right here in our local forests and sometimes even in our own backyards.

Some of the most commonly seen woodpeckers in the Pacific Northwest are the tiny downy woodpecker, the hairy woodpecker, the northern flicker, the red-breasted sapsucker, and the biggest of them all, the pileated woodpecker.

Red-breasted sapsuckers and northern flickers don't have "wood-pecker" in their name, but they're still members of the woodpecker family.

Who knew? If you banged your face on a tree all day, you'd get a concussion for sure. So why don't woodpeckers get brain damage? Well, that's something scientists are still studying. There's a lot to learn! So far they've noticed that the woodpecker's head is designed a little differently than other birds' heads. Their head bones are designed to squish a little to absorb impact, kind of like a helmet. They also have a bone in their

Pileated woodpecker

head (the hyoid, or tongue-bone) that keeps their brain from smash-ing up against the inside of their skull.

Downy Woodpecker

Male

Female

SIZE: The smallest North American woodpecker, the downy, is common throughout the Pacific Northwest. At 5½ to 6½ inches, it is barely bigger than a chickadee.

COLOR & PATTERN: This tiny woodpecker has a classic black-and-white woodpecker's body. It has black wings with white spots, a black back with a white streak, a white breast, and white stripes on the sides of its black head. Males also have a red patch at the back of their head. Pay close attention to those black spots on the white parts of the downy's tail too. That's one feature that will help you tell them apart from a hairy woodpecker, which doesn't have spots like that on its tail.

SOUND: *Tap! Tap! Tap! Tap!* Often, the best way to spot a woodpecker is to stand still and listen. The first thing you might hear is their repeated hammering on a nearby tree or snag. The downy woodpecker's tap is rapid—the taps are quick and close together. Their call is a high-pitched series of repeated scratchy notes that lasts about two seconds.

Like many birds, woodpeckers have a translucent (partly see-through) third eyelid called a nictitating membrane that they can pull across their eye to protect it. This is especially important as woodpeckers peck holes. It not only keeps wood chips and splinters from flying in, but it also keeps the birds' eyeballs from popping out.

Downy woodpecker's nictitating membrane

NEST & EGGS: Woodpeckers are the best-known cavity nesters out there. The holes they drill are later used by many other birds for their own nests. In the case of the downy, the male and female work together to drill out their nesting hole. The female downy lays three to eight small white eggs on the wood chips in the bottom of the cavity. Chicks hatch out naked and completely helpless.

FOOD: Downy woodpeckers eat mostly insects, but they'll also eat seeds and suet from feeders.

REGION & HABITAT: Downy woodpeckers are widespread across all of North America. They like open woodlands and human-created natural areas such as parks and orchards.

SEASON: Year-round.

Hairy Woodpecker

Male

Female

SIZE: These medium-sized woodpeckers range from around 7 to 10 inches long.

COLOR & PATTERN: No matter what the name says, this bird does not grow hair. It has feathers, just like all other birds. Early birders thought the white feathers going down the middle of its back looked like hair, so the name stuck.

The hairy woodpecker has the same colors and pattern as the smaller downy woodpecker—they are black and white all over, and the males have red patches on their heads—so many people have trouble telling the two apart.

When colors and patterns are the same, that means it's time for a birder to look at other field marks. First, check the size. A downy is much smaller than a hairy woodpecker. The hairy woodpecker is robin-sized, while a downy woodpecker is only a little bigger than a chickadee. The next thing to check is the bill. A hairy woodpecker's bill is thin, strong, and about as

Male hairy woodpecker (right) and juvenile male downy woodpecker (left)

Female hairy woodpecker (left) and juvenile male hairy woodpecker (right)

long as its head. A downy woodpecker's bill is much smaller, only about one-third as long as its head. Lastly, the downy has spots on the white parts of its tail, and the hairy does not. Look at the picture at left. One of these male woodpeckers is also much younger than the other (the downy is a juvenile), but the field marks are still pretty clear. *Can you see the differences?*

SOUND: The most common call made by this woodpecker is a sharp "peek" sound. More often, they'll drum their beaks on a tree to communicate, even when they're not trying to drill. Listen for a regular, quick knocking sound if you want to find a hairy woodpecker in the wild. Another other fun sound you may hear—especially if you see these birds in your yard—is the *bbbrrrr* sound their wings make when they get startled and fly away quickly (flush).

NEST & EGGS: Hairy woodpecker couples work together to drill out their nest. The female lays three to six white eggs per clutch. Babies are born helpless and mostly naked.

During breeding season mama birds need a lot of calcium to make all those egg shells. You can help birds out by putting clean crumbled eggshells outside near your feeders. After your family cooks eggs to eat, rinse off the shells and spread them on a pan. Bake in the oven at 250 degrees F for about 10 minutes to kill any bacteria that may harm the birds. Let cool, and then spread them outside, or put them in their own little feeder tray. Mama birds, like this hairy woodpecker, will happily eat these little pieces for the extra calcium in the shells.

FOOD: Like all woodpeckers, hairy woodpeckers are primarily insectivores. They can be a huge help in controlling pests like bark-boring beetles and caterpillars that eat the young leaves off of trees.

REGION & HABITAT: These common woodpeckers live all over most of North America. They like all kinds of trees and can be found in forests as well as suburban yards.

SEASON: Year-round.

Northern Flicker

Male

Female

SIZE: These are fairly big woodpeckers—bigger than a hairy but smaller than a pileated (you'll read about it next). They average between 11 and 12 inches long.

COLOR & PATTERN: Northern flickers are one of the easiest woodpeckers to identify. They have distinctive spotted bellies with a crisp black bib on their chest. Instead of black and white like our other local woodpeckers, northern flickers are a soft brown with black spots and bars. The males have a bright red "whisker" or mustache stripe on each cheek. The type of northern flicker that lives here in the Pacific Northwest is called a red-shafted northern flicker because the shaft (or center stalk) of its flight feathers is red. This makes it a beautiful bird to watch fly, as it flashes deep salmon-toned flight feathers that look like a flicker of firelight.

SOUND: Northern flickers make a loud call that sounds like a pileated woodpecker and/or a laughing monkey. It sounds a little like

"kwi-kwi-kwi-kwi-kwi." Especially during mating season, flickers like to make themselves heard by drumming. Flicker drumming is super-fast (like a drumroll), and they often like the sound they can make on something metal—like the gutter on a house. If you have flickers around your house, you may be awakened one day by an early-morning drumroll being played near your window.

Who knew? When a northern flicker drums, it may strike the tree (or your gutter or the side of your house) up to twenty-five times per second. That's fast!

NEST & EGGS: Flickers will drill out a nest cavity, but unlike many other woodpeckers, they'll also reuse a nest somebody else dug out in a previous year. (Why do all the work if you don't have to?) The female lays one clutch of five to eight eggs per year, and the babies hatch out naked and helpless.

Northern flicker fledglings look surprisingly like their parents. They look like they should be fending for themselves when the parents are still regurgitating food down their throats.

Northern flicker fledgling

Northern flicker male hunting for grubs

FOOD: Unlike other woodpeckers, these birds spend a lot of their time on the ground hunting for ants and beetles in the grass. They will still hunt and peck for insects on trees, but they're the only woodpecker you'll see pecking your lawn. Like many other woodpeckers, they will also visit feeders for both seeds and suet. (They particularly love suet.)

REGION & HABITAT: Northern flickers live all over North America. You can spot them in most types of woodlands here in the Pacific Northwest.

SEASON: These are year-round residents in most of the Northwest, and they're summer visitors in inland Canada and Alaska.

Pileated Woodpecker

Male

Female

SIZE: The largest woodpecker is the pileated (some people say "pie-lee-ated," others say "pill-e-ated"), and it averages up to around 19 inches long.

COLOR & PATTERN: Pileated woodpeckers are mostly black with white on their cheeks, neck, and under their wings. The most noticeable feature on both males and females is the bright red crest on top of their head. The males also have a red mustache.

SOUND: You can tell the pileated woodpecker's pecking thumps from other woodpeckers because they are deeper sounding and slower—less of a *tap tap tap tap tap*, and more of a *thunk . . . thunk . . . thunk*. They also have a laughing call that is similar to a northern flicker's.

NEST & EGGS: The male digs out most of the nest with the female doing the finishing touches at the end. She then lays one clutch of three to five eggs per year. The babies hatch out naked and helpless.

FOOD: At least half of these big birds' diet is made up of carpenter ants who are eating their way through rotting logs. Digging through the wood for the ants, pileated woodpeckers leave behind big rectangular holes that lots of other birds and animals use later for shelter and nesting. The rest of their diet is made up of other insects, wild berries, and nuts. If you're lucky enough to have a forest near your yard, you may even see them at your suet feeder.

REGION & HABITAT: This impressive woodpecker lives in the western part of the Pacific Northwest as well as throughout most of Canada and the eastern half of the United States. The large pileated woodpecker is most often found deep in mature forests. But they'll venture out to the suburbs for a big tree that promises a good ant feast.

SEASON: Year-round.

Red-breasted Sapsucker

SIZE: This is a medium-sized woodpecker, usually between 8 and 9 inches long. They're pretty stout birds, often looking a little chubbier than other woodpeckers.

COLOR & PATTERN: The folks who named this particular sapsucker may have been a little confused about bird body parts. It doesn't just have a red *breast*. Its whole *head* is red! If you see a woodpecker in the Pacific Northwest with a totally red head, odds are it's a red-breasted sapsucker. In this case, there's no tell-tale difference between the looks of the male and the female.

SOUND: Red-breasted sapsuckers have a call that sounds a lot like a dog's squeaky toy. It's a single, high-pitched squeaky "waah." You can also hear their drumming sounds—drumming is what birders call the sound woodpeckers make pecking on trees. The beats are pretty quick, and they have more irregular pauses than many other woodpeckers. *Peckpeck . . . peckpeckpeckpeckpeckpeck . . . peckpeckpeck.*

NEST & EGGS: Sapsuckers are cavity nesters like other woodpeckers. The female will lay four to seven eggs per clutch and has just one brood of chicks per year.

FOOD: Have you ever seen lines of tiny holes drilled across a tree trunk? Those are sapsucker holes! The sapsucker drills those dotted lines to tap the sweet sap running through the outer wood of a tree. It then eats both the sap and the insects that are drawn to it. You can see the little holes in the photo, and you can also see that the red-breasted sapsucker will also eat fruit.

Who knew? Humans eat sap too! Have you ever had real maple syrup? That's made from the sap of the maple tree. People gather it a lot like the sapsucker does, by drilling small holes in the side of maple trees.

REGION & HABITAT: Red-breasted sapsuckers can be found along the West Coast of North America all the way up into the very southern tip of Alaska. They breed in evergreen forests but enjoy the sweet sap of deciduous trees as well. Like other woodpeckers, they need dead snags for nesting.

SEASON: These birds live year-round along the Pacific coast and can be seen during the summertime farther inland.

Who knew? What other common Pacific Northwest bird likes to snack on sweetness? The hummingbird, of course! Some of those little fliers follow sapsuckers around to take a nibble or two of the sweet sap and attracted bugs after the bigger birds are through drilling the holes.

Bird-Safe Windows

One of the biggest threats humans pose to birds is completely unintentional: window strikes. Birds just don't understand glass windows. They will often fly full-speed into a window because what they see is reflected sky and trees. Up to a *billion* birds die this way every year in the United States alone. Birds sometimes also "fight" with their reflection, believing it's a rival bird in their territory.

There are a lot of easy ways to make windows safer for the birds in your yard. Local birding stores and online shops carry stickers, adhesive film, and other products you can put on your windows to help ward off birds. Here are a few do-it-yourself ideas to try as well.

1   Apply strips of tape (or lines of soap or tempera paint) on the outside of your window. Vertical lines 4 inches apart may be fine, but smaller birds may still try to fly through those "bars." The safest pattern if you have a window that gets a lot of smaller bird strikes is a grid with both vertical and horizontal lines.

2   Hang long pieces of heavy cord on the outside of your window, evenly spaced around 4 inches apart.

3   Install a screen or netting on the outside of your window.

4   Close a door between your rooms to remove the illusion that a bird can fly straight through your house.

If a bird does strike your window, check to see if it's okay. If it has an obvious injury like a broken wing, have an adult call a trained wild-life rehabilitator. Your local Audubon Society or the internet may be able to suggest some-one who can help. If the  bird seems okay but is dazed, place it somewhere safe and keep your pets inside while it recovers. Do not try to do more than that without proper training.

Trained wildlife rehabilitators help thousands of birds every year. They know what each species needs if it's too young or too hurt to be on its own. Find out more about the wildlife rehab centers near you and how you can support them. When you get older, you could even be a volunteer or on-site biologist to help with the important work they do.

Cedar waxwings

Acknowledgments

A huge thank-you to all the people who helped me hatch this book. So many supported and added to this project as it grew. Michelle McCann gave my original idea wings. Christy Cox and all the editors, designers, and staff at Little Bigfoot and Sasquatch Books gave it feathers and helped it fledge. Delaney Pearson turned birdsong into musical notation. Cary Porter made gorgeous art out of a bone chart and bird bums. Maddy Reid sent a lovely photo of a European robin from across the pond. Richmond and Lori dissected owl pellets like expert archaeologists. Kaylee and Quinn mixed up a bird-tasty batch of suet. Cathy made me coffee while letting me stalk crows on her birdbath. Jesse drove on avian safaris and found me feathers. Tonya let me photograph her grumpy cat and amazing catio. My dad joined me on adventures in search of owls and bluebirds. Mom cheered me on and fed the yard-birds while I was away. Austin and Caden gave me enthusiastic support and honest, intelligent feedback. Angel, Jen, Karla, Alicia, and Karen listened (and listened) as I talked through the process, embracing my bird nerdiness with patience, affection, and even secret intel on schoolyard screech-owls.

And finally, I need to give a special enormous thank-you to my amazingly supportive husband, Eric, who works hard every day so I can follow my dreams.

Glossary

Adaptation: a physical feature or behavior that helps an animal survive in the wild

Alert: the way birds warn each other that danger is near

Anting: an unusual feather care activity in which birds let ants crawl on their feathers or rub ants on their bodies

Barring: striped horizontal markings, often on the breast

Bird blind: an artificial screen used to hide birders so they can watch without frightening the birds

Bird calls: shorter cheeps, whistles, tweets, and other noises that help birds communicate with each other

Bird songs: usually, but not always, a more complicated set of sounds made by certain types of birds, often used to mark territory or attract mates (in some bird species, only the male sings)

Birders: birdwatchers (informal)

Brood: a family of birds all born from a single clutch of eggs

Brood parasites: birds who lay their eggs in other birds' nests

Camouflage: using colors or patterns to help you blend into your surroundings, and a way in which birds and other animals conceal themselves in their natural environment

Carrion: the flesh of dead animals

Cavity nesters: birds that live in holes in trees, rocks, or other structures

Cere: a bald fleshy area at the base of some birds' beaks that contains the nostrils

Clutch: a group of eggs produced by a bird at one time

Coniferous trees: trees that have cones and needles

Contact call: the sound birds make while they're flying or feeding to keep track of other members of their flock

Corvid: a bird in the animal family Corvidae, including crows, ravens, jays, rooks, jackdaws, magpies, treepies, choughs, and nutcrackers

Covey: a group of quail

Crop: a pouch in the throat where a bird can temporarily store extra food

Dabbling: a type of feeding by ducks that involves tipping their back end up with their head in the water

Deciduous trees: trees that lose their leaves seasonally, typically in the fall

Down: the fluffy underlayer of feathers that keep birds warm

Duckling: a baby duck

Eaglet: a baby eagle

Edge: a space where two different types of habitat meet

Evergreen trees: trees that stay green year-round

Falconer: a person who trains and works with raptors

Field guide: a book that helps you identify plants, animals, and other features in nature

Field marks: details that help you identify a bird (these can range from size, pattern, and color to behaviors such as what a bird eats or how it flies)

Fledge: to leave the nest; to develop flying feathers

Fledgling: a young bird who has left the nest but may not yet know how to fly

Flock: a big group of birds; can also be a verb meaning to gather together

Flush: to take off flying; fly away quickly

Gape: the inside of a bird's mouth, which is soft and bright on baby birds to aid in feeding

Gape flange: the fleshy area where the two halves of the beak join

Gizzard: the strongly muscled part of a bird's stomach that grinds up its food

Gleaner: a bird that picks tiny insects and mites off of leaves

Gosling: a baby goose

Guano: bird poop (the term is also used for the poop of reptiles)

Hackles: long feathers on the throat of a raven; can also refer to certain hairs on a mammal

Hatchling: a newly hatched baby bird

Herbivore: a plant eater

Hummer: birder speak for hummingbird

Incubate: keep eggs warm

Insectivore: an animal that eats primarily insects

Iridescent: shines with different colors in the light

Juvenile: not yet adult

Keratin: a type of protein that makes up human hair, fingernails, and toenails, as well as birds' beaks and feathers

Lamprey: an eel-like sucker fish eaten by fishing birds

LBB: little brown bird

Leucistic: having a partial loss of color in the feathers

Life list (or lifer list): a running list kept by birders of all of the birds they see

Migration: moving long distances seasonally to feed or reproduce

Molting: losing old feathers and growing new ones

Mottled: spotted or splotched

Murder: a group of crows

Murmuration: a bloblike flock of starlings

Naturalist: a person who studies nature

Nestling: a baby bird who hasn't left the nest

Nictitating membrane: a translucent (partly see-through) third eyelid on birds, reptiles, and some mammals

Nocturnal: active at night

Non-native species: an animal or plant that is found in but is not originally from a certain area

Omnivore: an animal that eats both plants and animals

Opportunistic eaters: a bird or other animal that will eat whatever it can find with the least amount of effort

Ornithologists: scientists who study birds

Owlet: baby owl

Pin feathers: feathers that are not yet fully developed

Plumage: a bird's feathers collectively

Preening: the behaviors birds use to care for their feathers

Prey: animals that are hunted and eaten by other animals

Raptor: a bird of prey

Roost: when birds sleep for the night; also a noun describing where they sleep (birds *roost* on a *roost*)

Scavengers: animals that eat primarily dead things (carrion)

Shaft: the main central "trunk" of a feather

Snag: a dead tree

Talons: sharp, hooked claws at the end of a bird's toes (especially a bird of prey)

Thicket: a group of bushes or small trees

Trill: a longer sound that vibrates between two notes

Understory: the plants below the main trees of a forest, often bushes and low-lying plants

Uric acid: a big component of bird pee that is very hard to dissolve; the white part of a bird's poop

Vertebrate: an animal with a backbone

Index

About the Author

Karen DeWitz is a nature-loving photographer, editor, former teacher, and bird nerd. Her happy place is a nest of blankets on her porch, where she can watch and photograph the more than fifty species of birds that visit her yard. Her two fledgling sons now work and go to school on opposite coasts. She lives in Oregon City with her husband and a shaggy dog who doesn't really understand watching birds if you're not planning on chasing them.